SUPERNATURAL BELIEVING

THE

CONSCIOUSNESS OF CHRIST

L. EMERSON FERRELL

International

SUPERNATURAL BELIEVING
The Consciousness of Christ

All scripture quotations unless otherwise indicated are taken from the King James version.

Cover design:
Ruben Mariaca Asport
rubenmariaca@yahoo.com

Interior design:
1106 Design
michele@1106design.com

Printing:
United Graphics, Inc.

Publisher:
E & A International
PO Box 3418
Ponte Vedra, Florida, 32004 USA
www.voiceofthelight.com

ISBN 978-1-933163-13-0

Content

Foreword

There have been many books released on the subject of faith in the last twenty years. The Lord has been challenging the church in this area because "without faith it is impossible to please God." There are still areas of unbelief in the church that must be challenged. Emerson Ferrell has always thought outside the box. He has been able to look at scripture and challenge us to think in a fresh way.

The Holy Spirit is our teacher. He is faithful to teach us the important truths we need to know in order to fulfill the will of God. He anoints men and women to minister and give the church knowledge and understanding. Emerson Ferrell has spent quality time praying and fasting to unlock the secrets of the word of God. This book is the fruit of that time spent. With the help of the Holy Spirit he has written a new book that will help the reader break free from the bondage of unbelief. Consider what he is saying, and the Lord will give you understanding in all things.

Emerson Ferrell has a desire to see the church walk in the supernatural. Signs and wonders are one of the marks of the apostolic calling. There are many who claim they believe without showing any proof. The problem is often with our way of thinking. Religious spirits affect the way we think. Jesus was not "religious" enough for the leaders of his generation. He was anointed. The anointing affected the way he thought and ministered. The same is true today. Allow the anointing upon this book to challenge any thinking that is hindering you from walking in the fullness of power and authority. I pray that you will be released apostolically to do the greater works of Jesus Christ.

—JOHN ECKHARDT
December, 2006

Introduction

The world has become a place of increasing uncertainty. It is rare to see a television newscast whose lead stories do not contain death and destruction. The appetite for increasingly sensational news seems to be the diet of the world. The media is shaping the reality of the world, while maintaining that it reports the truth.

The question one should ask is what determines our reality; our belief or someone else's. The answer to that question will require answering another question. If reality is according to our belief, then what is our source or substance of reality? The substance of anything is the inner material, which forms the outer condition.

If there is one word in a universal vocabulary used most frequently to validate our behavior it is *believe*. For example, comments such as *I believe this is the truth* or *I do not believe you* represent an opinion or an attitude that determines a course of action in a person's life.

Our most important decisions are determined typically by information we believe or do not believe. The age in which we live is full of information. In fact, many refer to this century as the *information age* because of the variety of ways we are exposed to data.

Perhaps no other word in the world is more critical to a Christian's vocabulary than the word believe. Think about it: our belief determines what system or person to follow. Perhaps this is why the term believer predominately refers to Christians or other religious organizations.

One of the purposes of this book is to expose our minds to a new understanding of a common word, believe. **The Holy Spirit is capable of changing the common for the supernatural if we will give Him free access to our preconceived ideas.**

For example, in the fifteenth century, people believed that the world was flat. This belief instilled fear in all those who wanted to sail the oceans or explore new lands. We are all guilty of building belief systems around false information, and the results are often tragic. Today, there are thousands of Muslims who believe they will not only go to heaven but also be rewarded for killing those who do not share their belief. Terror grips the world because of this insane belief.

The world is looking for answers to solve this crisis but the world, as we will discover, is unable to solve problems with a belief system born from the same sin nature.

Belief in anything or anyone is one of the key dynamics in motivating, mobilizing and establishing groups of people throughout the earth. Another dynamic, which connects with belief, is reward. It is common knowledge most people will change their belief if what they believe does not reward them or produce what they want.

All Christians assume they believe in God. Do we? The Bible says something very important to consider in James.

> You **believe** that there is one God. That's fine! The **demons also believe** that, and they tremble with fear.
> JAMES 2:19

Humans are not the only species capable of believing. Demons also believe, and in this case, it produces a response, trembling. When is the last time we trembled at the knowledge of God? This book will stir you, challenge you, shake and enlighten you in order to turn you into a powerful, miracle-working believer.

Beloved, if you are content with your life and have everything from God you need or want, this book is not for you. However, if there is a burning discontent inside you that is screaming for more of the Holy Spirit, do not stop until that scream turns to rejoicing.

Chapter One

Centers of Belief

1. WHAT IS IT TO BELIEVE?

I cannot tell you how many times I have heard the phrase "believe me." Each time I hear it; something inside me questions the sincerity or truthfulness of the one who is making the statement. This happens for a reason, as we will learn in the next section. However, typically, we give the person saying it the benefit of the doubt unless experiences have proven otherwise.

Of course, all those who are parents have used this phrase many times and as a rule have tried their best to remain credible and trustworthy to their children. Nevertheless, the first time parents fail to deliver on the promise associated with those words, the children's confidence wanes, followed by doubt and unbelief.

I think it would be wise to look at scriptures to examine more closely the word believe.

> *When He reached the house and went in, the blind men came to Him, and Jesus said to them, Do you **believe** that I am able to do this? They said to Him, Yes, Lord.*
> MATTHEW 9:28

The following two illustrations in Mark describe the most common ways of believing as it relates to the invisible and visible kingdoms. In order to enter the invisible kingdom of God, **repentance is the requirement**, which allows one to believe. **Repent** means to change the way you think. The visible kingdom is comprised of people who primarily believe if they can feel, touch, taste, hear or see.

> *...and saying, the time is fulfilled, and the kingdom of God is at hand; **repent** and **believe** in the gospel.*
> MARK 1:15

> *Let this Christ, the King of Israel, now come down from the cross, so that we may **see** and **believe**!*
> MARK 15:32

The choice to believe or not to believe is always ours, as shown in the following scriptures.

> *And when they heard that He was alive, and had been seen by her, they refused to **believe** it.*
> MARK 16:11

> *And they went away and reported it to the others, but they did not **believe** them either.*
> MARK 16:13

> *If You are the Christ, tell us. But He said to them, If I tell you, you will not **believe**.*
> LUKE 22:67

This amazing statement is as true today as it was two thousand years ago. The truth of that statement separates those who believe according to this world's system and those who repent according to this world's belief system.

*God loved the world this way: He gave his only Son so that everyone who **believes** in him will not die but will have eternal life.*

JOHN 3:16

*Those who **believe** in him won't be condemned. But those who don't **believe** are already condemned because they **don't believe** in God's only Son.*

JOHN 3:18

*And all things, whatsoever ye shall ask in prayer, **believing**, ye shall receive.*

MATTHEW 21:22

Faith is used in place of believing in every other translation but the King James, which is very significant. **Believing, according to my definition, is a "continuous knowing."**

*Whoever **believes** in the Son has eternal life, but whoever rejects the Son will not see life. Instead, he will see God's constant anger.*

JOHN 3:36

*Of Him all the prophets bear witness that through His name everyone who **believes** in Him receives forgiveness of sins.*

ACTS 10:43

7

> *You are My witnesses, declares the LORD, And My*
> *servant whom I have chosen, **In order that you may***
> ***know and believe Me, And understand that I am***
> ***He.** Before Me there was no God formed, And there will*
> *be none after Me.*
>
> ISAIAH 43:10

The verse in Isaiah is God's blueprint for all of us who want to believe Him. We must first *know* Him in order to understand Him. So how do you get to know God? The same way that you learn about anyone: spend time with that person. If you want to know God, study and examine Jesus, the visible image of God.

It is obvious from the few verses quoted that the word **believe** is important. Faith and believe are used over three hundred times in the Bible. Nevertheless, Jesus made no distinction between either word.

Some languages today, such as German and Dutch, use the same word for faith and believe. This practice alone has made the Bible no different from any other book one reads and chooses to believe or not to believe. This reduces the supernatural power of the words of Christ to a mental understanding.

Therefore, it is even more critical to understand the context in which Jesus describes the word **believes.** Our study will demonstrate why Jesus had results. The reasons for this will become clear as we explore the different centers of our being.

The life that we are living now is the result of what and whom we believe. The majority of the people who will read this book consider themselves Christians. However, we should know why we are Christians and what makes our belief superior to every other belief system on the planet.

We should set goals so that this book can be a tool the Holy Spirit uses to join our spirits with His.

Our primary goal should be to individually understand what the word believe means as it relates to our life and relationship with Christ.

DEFINITIONS OF BELIEVE

Believe is defined in two different ways. The first is how the Bible uses believe while the second is a more popular or secular definition and most frequently used by the average Christian.

- *To accept as true or real, to credit with authenticity; to have firm faith, especially religious faith; to have confidence, or trust; to have confidence in the truth; to regard (something) as true or real; to trust what one has seen or heard and to have an opinion; think.*

- *In popular use and familiar discourse, to believe often expresses an opinion in a vague manner, without a very exact estimate of evidence, noting a mere preponderance of opinion, and is nearly equivalent to think or suppose.*

According to these definitions, observe the way that most Christians use the word believe. In Charismatic circles, we hear proclamations such as **"I am believing for** my healing, car, finances, wife..." In general, these "confessions," imply a future manifestation. Faith is most often associated with this kind of proclamation or declaration. **We must ask ourselves whether this is the correct use of the word believe in relation to faith.** The Bible says, *"Now faith is..."* which means presently, not in the future.

Most of us have heard many faith messages, and some of us know the definition by rote. However, at this point we will examine two translations and later go into detail.

*Now faith is the substance of things **hoped for**, the evidence of things not seen.*

HEBREWS 11:1 (KING JAMES VERSION)

Faith assures us of things we expect and convinces us of the existence of things we cannot see.

HEBREWS 11:1 (GOD'S WORD TRANSLATION)

Most teachers attempt to make the distinction between what they call Bible hope and worldly hope. Most say that Bible hope implies assurance and confidence but the secular world uses hope with uncertainty and doubt. I think this is a true and accurate description.

Unfortunately, in our zeal to maintain what some call "a good confession," we often use the word believing in a context more identified with the secular definition ("equivalent to think or suppose").

For example, if someone prays for a person who is sick, without any change, the sick person might say, if asked about his or her condition, "I am believing for my healing". This would seem to indicate their condition has not changed, but they hope it does in the future. That would be like saying "I am a seeker of the truth."

They are looking for the answer and *hope* to find it one day. *Seekers are not finders.* Furthermore, they have been trained to believe only what they can see, touch or feel. **The soul is the home to such emotions, senses and physical experiences and is not the center where faith resides.**

Jesus used believing in Matthew 21:22, according to the King James Version, but it is translated as faith in the Amplified, New Revised Standard and Weymouth Bibles.

*And all things, whatsoever ye shall ask in prayer, **believing**, ye shall receive.*

MATTHEW 21:22

*And all things, whatever you make request for in prayer, having **faith**, you will get.*

NEW REVISED STANDARD

*Whatever you ask for in prayer with **faith**, you will receive.*

WEYMOUTH

2. BELIEVING FROM THE SPIRIT

The manner in which Jesus believed was with His spirit. His faith was the trust that He formed by observing His Father. Therefore, He developed His mind by watching His Father. So His believing and faith were married in His spirit in order to produce the visible manifestation of the thing for which he prayed. That was because His spirit, soul, and body were one inside the Father. Did He not say that He and His Father were one?

Our problem is that we believe from a soul whose condition is like that of the first Adam. Understanding this is our challenge, but the fruit of this knowledge will make us supernatural believers.

Our final goal is to reconnect our soul with the mind of Christ. In other words, Adam's fall disconnected his spirit from the Father and one of the consequences was to doom all men to believing in their souls.

Sin will always veil the truth, and the results are predictable: man will establish catastrophic belief systems. Therefore, the more exposed we are to truth, the more likely we are to trust Jesus and **believe Him**.

Darkness controls our thoughts and ultimately our beliefs because of man's fall. **The truth is, each time our decisions exclude Jesus and exalt self Adam's treason is on display in our own life**.

11

The words that portray the Bible's meaning of believe are "truth and trust." The importance of these words will become crucial as we develop the next goal of our discussion, which is **why we believe certain things and reject others**. The answer to this question will expose all of us to the measure in which the Holy Spirit directs our spirits.

For example, ten years ago I was unable to trust the Holy Spirit to fast for three days, whereas now I trust Him for whatever He asks as it relates to fasting.

Rejecting my false belief system, constructed from fear and wrong information, and consciously trusting the Holy Spirit changed my believing. This simple trust has helped me tremendously to hear the Holy Spirit more clearly.

Fasting has helped me to reject many false structures in my believing and increased my faith to believe for the supernatural.

As a first step in your journey to believe like Jesus, begin trusting the Holy Spirit in the places where you have developed confidence and faith. He may have healed and delivered you or blessed you financially.

Regardless, begin to expand your faith and belief for a miracle in those areas where the devil has lied to you. Start trusting the Holy Spirit for more miracles in your life. The more you trust Him, the more strength you will obtain to overcome the enemy and be set free, in Jesus' name.

3. BELIEF CENTER MOVED TO THE SOUL

Adam's fall relocated the belief center from his spirit to his soul for all mankind.

Investigating the way that we believe requires us to start at the place of all origins, Genesis. God made man in His image and likeness. That means all of us are created to rule, reign as "spirits" and believe like our heavenly Father.

Then God said, "Let Us make man in Our image, according to Our likeness; and let them rule over the fish of the sea and over the birds of the sky and over the cattle and over all the earth, and over every creeping thing that creeps on the earth." God created man in His own image, in the image of God He created him; male and female He created them.

GENESIS 1:26–27

God created man to rule and have dominion over everything on and in the earth, except other men. **God, who is spirit, designed man's spirit as the apparatus to receive His instructions.**

God determined to create a race of God Sons on the earth whose purpose was to establish and maintain His kingdom. This required Sons who would believe like their Father. **The failure of the first Adam is a continuing saga of man's inability to choose correctly whom to believe.** The wrong choice resulted in separating mans spirit from God thereby exalting the soul to a position replacing God.

And the man and his wife were both naked and were not ashamed.
Now the serpent was craftier than any beast of the field, which the LORD God had made. And he said to the woman, indeed, has God said, 'You shall not eat from any tree of the garden'?
The woman said to the serpent, "From the fruit of the trees of the garden we may eat; but from the fruit of the tree which is in the middle of the garden, God has said, 'you shall not eat from it or touch it, or you will die."
The serpent said to the woman, "You surely will not die! "For God knows that in the day you eat from it

13

*your eyes will be opened, and **you will be like God,
knowing good and evil.***"

GENESIS 3:1–5

God created Adam both male and female before separating the two. It was after the division when the serpent posed the question to the woman: *And he said to the woman, indeed, has God said, "You shall not eat from any tree of the garden"?*

One of the greatest deceptions of the enemy is to make you and me believe we are God. For example, how often have you heard people say, "If there was a God, He certainly would not allow such a catastrophe," or "How can God permit so many deaths from storms?"

These questions sound holy and righteous but are in reality a deliberate perversion of the authority and sovereignty of God. **How arrogant it is for the created to question the creator**. However, many of our beliefs originate from the same lofty prideful position equal to or usurping the authority of God.

As the dialogue continues between the woman and the devil, it becomes obvious that her soul was engaged in making the damning decisions. The devil had successfully created doubt and unbelief. However, more importantly, he had appealed to the senses of the soul to make the decision. **The soul primarily wants power, emotional security, wisdom and wealth. Once she believed the lie, her soul could justify any action.**

*When the woman saw that the tree was good for food, and that it was a delight to the eyes, and that the tree was **desirable to make one wise**, she took from its fruit and ate; and she gave also to her husband with her, and he ate. Then the eyes of both of them were* *opened, and* **they knew that they were naked;** *and they sewed fig leaves together and made themselves loin coverings.*

GENESIS 3:6–7

The truth is, spiritual decisions are not the function of our soul. The soul is to believe and act according to our spirits. The spirit is the source of faith and power, whereas the soul is the magnificent tool God created to manifest from faith, believing into the senses, will and emotions.

Adam chose not to believe God, and the result is the sin nature. This produces a consciousness, a way of thinking contrary to God, which we will now discuss in detail.

Chapter Two

Sin Consciousness versus Christ Consciousness

1. SIN CONSCIOUSNESS

Before accepting Christ as my Lord, I experimented with hallucinogenic drugs. The instant my mind was intoxicated I began to doubt everything. I was paranoid and skeptical about most things, questioning everything I had learned as a child from the scriptures, including Jesus as the Son of God. I was the most important person, and could rationalize just about anything. For example, if I wanted a good grade in school but did not want to study, I could justify cheating to achieve it. Anyone who did not agree with my philosophy and belief system was my enemy.

The hallucinogenic state and sin consciousness have many characteristics in common. Self, ego and pride are the dynamics, which sustain one's doubts and paranoia. Fear becomes your closest ally and is the driving force behind all decisions. **Sin separates man from the truth and light. Therefore, where there is no truth or light, believing a lie is easy.**

Believing and faith were one in Adam because his spirit and soul were one with God. In other words, before Adam disobeyed God his spirit was the authority over the earth or visible realm. **Adam's original condition is the model for faith. His spirit and soul believed and the invisible became visible.**

One of the most monumental tragedies that occurred from Adam's betrayal was that the center for believing moved from the spirit to the soul. **Sin dethroned the spirit and crowned the intellect. Once the intellectual side of man is exalted, sin is unleashed and dominates every department of man.**

The shift from the spirit to the soul in Adam is obvious when we compare Genesis 2:25 and 3:7. *And the man and his wife were **both naked and were not ashamed.** Then the eyes of both of them were opened, and **they knew that they were naked**; and they sewed fig leaves together and made themselves loin coverings.*

When I refer to the spirit of man, I am speaking about the invisible container or shell, with the capacity to be full of God or the devil. In contrast, the soul is the magnificent apparatus designed by God to connect our spirits and bodies. This mechanism includes the emotions, will and mind. **(Refer to figures 1 & 2 on pages 133 and 134)**

Sin creates a consciousness or knowledge of shame and guilt. Many believe that sin is what man thinks. **Sin is not what we think it is what God has determined it to be.** We think and believe from our conscience, while God thinks from His. God's faith and belief are from the purity of His nature. Man thinks, believes and acts according to the impurity of his conscious soul, which we know is sinful from birth.

Definitions for the word **consciousness** are: *knowledge of one's own existence, condition, sensations, mental operations, acts, etc. the reality or awareness by the mind of itself and the world. Another way of explaining consciousness is the **knowledge of right and wrong** according to the soul. Alternatively, one might say, consciousness is what **the soul knows that it knows**. Consciousness can be a **subjective awareness** of the aspects of cognitive processing and the* *content of the mind. Furthermore, it can be **attitudes and feelings** of an individual or of a group of people.*

Simply stated, consciousness is the way we think and believe from our experiences and knowledge.

A **belief system describes a structure of believing** that may or may not be true and produces a behavior constructed from information or material either visible or invisible.

For example, during the fifteenth century most of the population believed the world was flat. That wrong belief shaped the consciousness or thinking of that age. **Believing is to consciousness as a potter's hand is to the clay. Therefore, what we believe determines the reality we perceive.**

In other words, the knowledge we believe will determine our behavior, regardless if the information is true or false, as illustrated in the above example. This is what happened in the Garden of Eden. Regrettably, that treachery was a permanent separation from God, and **the result is a sin consciousness for all mankind.**

The following definitions describe conscience, which is the root word for consciousness.

Conscience is: *behavior according to what your sense of right and wrong tells you is right or a person's moral sense of right and wrong, chiefly as it affects his or her own behavior. (Motivation deriving logically from ethical or moral principles that govern a person's thoughts and actions.)*

The serpent told the woman, "Your eyes would be opened and you would be as God, knowing good and evil." God told the man that the day he eats of the fruit "he would surely die." **Man chose to believe the lie, and his behavior resulted in the death of his God consciousness.**

> *Unto the pure all things are pure: but unto them that are defiled and unbelieving is nothing pure; but even their mind and conscience is defiled.*
>
> TITUS 1:15

19

Purity is the substance of innocence; sin conscience is the substance of unbelief.

In my opinion, the conscience resides between our spirits and souls, like a bridge. **(See figure 2 on page 134)**

I believe it is God's divine homing device with a built-in loudspeaker for calling us back home. Unfortunately, the more we ignore His beckoning, the fainter His voice will become.

However, responding to His call convicts us of sin and opens our heart to the salvation process by the Holy Spirit. Later in the book, I will go into detail about salvation.

Once we understand the magnitude of our corruption, **relocating the center for believing back to our spirit will become our passion and priority.** One purpose of this book is to expose our spirits to this truth and thereby allow the Holy Spirit to destroy the false belief systems constructed by our souls.

> *Everyone who commits sin is guilty of lawlessness; sin is lawlessness.*
>
> 1 JOHN 3:4

Lawlessness is the result of man's disobedience in the Garden of Eden. The definition of lawlessness is detached or broken relationship and responsibility. Man lost his relationship with his Father, God. Therefore, he was unable to fulfill his responsibility of creating a race of God Sons on the earth.

Lawlessness is man's rebellion against his fundamental purpose at creation for relationship and responsibility (i.e., his relationship to God, his Father, and his responsibility to all mankind).

Once God expelled Adam and Eve from the Garden, the sin consciousness became rampant throughout creation, starting with their own son Cain. Total depravity spread among mankind, causing God to repent for creating man. This resulted in the destruction by flood of every living creature except Noah and his family.

> *The Lord asked Cain, Where is your brother Abel? I don't know, he answered.* **Am I supposed to take care of my brother?**
>
> GENESIS 4:9

The response of Cain to God after killing his brother is the attitude of everyone operating from a sin consciousness. **The sin consciousness is the mother of lawlessness in all human beings.**

> *The Lord saw that the wickedness of man was great in the earth, and that every imagination and intention of all human thinking was* **only evil continually.**
> *And the Lord regretted that He had made man on the earth, and He was grieved at heart.*
> *So the Lord said, I will destroy, blot out, and wipe away mankind, whom I have created from the face of the ground—not only man, [but] the beasts and the creeping things and the birds of the air—**for it grieves Me and makes Me regretful that I have made them.***
> *But Noah found grace (favor) in the eyes of the Lord.*
>
> GENESIS 6:5–8

No one knows the limits of consciousness available to the mind and spirit. **We have been slow to realize that man is a spirit and even slower to understand what a spirit is capable of believing.** We have educated the soul and magnified the intellectual and physical and in so doing unleashed the sin consciousness throughout all cultures. **This has produced a generation of self-seeking and self-centered beings whose only motivation for believing is self.**

21

The earth is full of lawlessness, and the helplessness of man is evident on a worldwide scale. The earthquakes and tsunamis are some of the results of the sin consciousness in the earth. This planet needs the Sons of God to arise now as never before, because the future of mankind is in the balance. Because of Adam's disobedience, we are living on an earth with a curse — as can be seen in the following scriptures.

> *And to Adam he said, Because you gave ear to the voice of your wife and took of the fruit of the tree which I said you were not to take, **the earth is cursed** on your account; in pain you will get your food from it all your life.*
>
> GENESIS 3:17

God cursed the snake, the woman and then the earth. The earth was flooded and all life destroyed but the curse remains. This planet is reeling and vomiting from the sin consciousness of lawless man. In my opinion, the hurricanes, floods, volcanoes and other catastrophes are not the result of greenhouse gases or freak weather patterns, but arise from the consciousness of sin throughout the earth. These are the sounds spoken of by Paul in Romans 8:18–23.

> *For all creation, gazing eagerly as if with outstretched neck, is waiting and longing to see the manifestation of the sons of God. For the Creation fell into subjection to failure and **unreality** (not of its own choice, but by the will of Him who so subjected it). Yet there was always the hope that at last the Creation itself would also be set free from the servitude of decay so as to enjoy the liberty that will attend the glory of the children of God. For we know that the whole of **Creation is groaning together in the pains of childbirth until this hour.***
>
> ROMANS 8:18–23

The miracle realm is man's natural realm. He is by creation the companion of the miracle-working God. Sin deposed man from that position, and the earth is groaning for the Sons of God to manifest. Paul is speaking about the childbirth, which results from the spirits and souls joined in Christ. The challenge for man today is the same as it was in the Garden; whom do you believe?

2. CHRIST CONSCIOUSNESS

A. HIS ASCENSION INTO THE CONSCIOUSNESS OF GOD

I want to be very clear about this subject. Christ consciousness is to sin consciousness as diamonds are to coal. It is not the opposite but a dimension beyond. For example, many extraordinary men and women have died for family and loved ones, but Jesus died for those who put Him to death. This demonstrates a consciousness few ever attain. Jesus achieved this level in God to demonstrate to all the powers and principalities in the universe, His kingship.

In order to believe like Jesus, we must follow His ascension into the consciousness of God. First, it must be obvious to anyone who has read the words of our Lord that He did not think or speak like others in His day.

Second, He did not say things in order to appeal to the poor and fight against the traditional belief structures. His mind was not conformed to the consciousness of the world. He spoke differently because He believed from the principles of heaven. He said in John 8:28, *I can't do anything on my own. Instead, I speak as the Father taught me.* Jesus had to depend on the words and lessons of His Father. Oh beloved, the secret of dominion is in that statement.

According to Hebrews 2:16 and 4:15 Jesus came to earth all God in His spirit but was, body and soul, the seed of Abraham.

For verily he took not on him the nature of angels; but he took on him the seed of Abraham.

HEBREWS 2:16

For we do not have a high priest who cannot sympathize with our weaknesses, but One who has been tempted in all things as we are, yet without sin.

HEBREWS 4:15

Clearly, Jesus was born in a world controlled by the consciousness of Adam or lawlessness. Man does not have to succumb to darkness, which Jesus demonstrated. Moreover, through **believing** the words of His Father a **Godman** could dominate. This first happened in the wilderness where He met the devil face to face.

Jesus was born the Son of God but not the savior of the world. This may shock some of you, but read what Paul writes in Hebrews.

Although He was God's Son, yet He learned obedience from the sufferings, which He endured; and so, having been made perfect, He became to all who obey Him the source and giver of eternal salvation.

HEBREWS 5:8–9

Some of you may say, "I have been quoting scripture the way Jesus did, but the devil is still destroying my life and family." Do not despair, your heavenly Father has not forsaken you, and today salvation has come to your situations. Believing as Jesus is the power to set you free and empower you to be more than an overcomer.

Jesus did not just quote scriptures but allowed the words to resonate from His very cells. For example, when He told the devil "do not tempt the Lord your God," I believe that every cell in His body was invisibly prostrate at the holiness of that statement.

In other words, the purity of God's words connected His spirit with His soul and body. There was no room for doubt and unbelief to uproot that command as it did the first Adam.

Someone once asked me what I thought was the primary reason to become a Christian. I said without hesitation, "to establish the kingdom of God in the world." Some people might say it is to avoid hell and others will say in order to go to heaven. I believe both of those are selfish. Jesus described His mission in Matthew.

> *Do not think that I came to abolish the Law or the Prophets; I did not come to abolish but to fulfill. For truly I say to you, until heaven and earth pass away, not the smallest letter or stroke shall pass from the Law until all is accomplished.*
> *Whoever then annuls one of the least of these commandments, and teaches others to do the same, shall be called least in the kingdom of heaven; but whoever keeps and teaches them, he shall be called great in the kingdom of heaven.*
>
> MATTHEW 5:17–19

Jesus studied the scriptures to understand completely the picture and character of who He was to become. He would find the scriptures from the prophets and meditate on them until every cell in His being became the words. His soul and body had to display the same righteousness and holiness of His spirit.

B. STEP ONE: RIGHTEOUSNESS THROUGH BAPTISM

The law was to show man a picture of the Christ in righteousness. Jesus came to fulfill in the flesh what the prophets foretold. When John baptized Jesus at the river Jordan, all of heaven was watching.

> *But Jesus made answer, saying to him, Let it be so now:*
> *because so it is right for us to* ***make righteousness***
> ***complete****. Then he gave him baptism.*
> *And Jesus, having been given baptism, straight away*
> *went up from the water; and, the heavens opening, he*
> *saw the Spirit of God coming down on him as a dove;*
> *And a voice came out of heaven, saying, This is my*
> *dearly loved Son, with whom I am well pleased.*
> MATTHEW 3:15–17

Jesus made His decision to fulfill the law or all righteousness beginning with baptism. He choose total consecration and now He was determined to complete His assignment, even His death on the cross. Then His Father, speaking audibly, confirmed His decision.

Baptism is one of the most fundamentally misunderstood requirements of anyone whose intent is to follow Christ. It is much more than obedience to a doctrine or religion. Jesus made only one command and method concerning baptism.

> *So wherever you go, make disciples of all nations:*
> ***Baptize them in the name of the Father, and of***
> ***the Son, and of the Holy Spirit.***
> MATTHEW 28:19

This was the only command He gave to His disciples concerning baptism. In essence, He was telling His disciples to immerse those who qualified as disciples into the character of the Father, Son and the Holy Spirit. **Baptism is the exchange of our spirit, soul and body into the Godhead**. This is total immersion into the character and personalities of God.

Although baptism is symbolic in the natural state, it is a heavenly design that prepares us for spiritual impartation.

Pay close attention to the requirements of a disciple. Look with me at Luke 14:26–27, 33 because meeting these qualifications is essential for our journey to obtain the mind of Christ.

> *If people come to me and are not ready to abandon their fathers, mothers, wives, children, brothers, and sisters, as well as their own lives, they cannot be my disciples. Therefore, those who do not carry their crosses and follow me cannot be my disciples. In the same way, none of you can be my disciples unless you give up everything.*
>
> Luke 14:26–27, 33

This is the requirement for becoming His disciple, spoken by Jesus Himself. Many enter into baptism and **believe** they are Christians but according to the words of our Lord do not qualify. Discipleship is a prominent position that demands specific characteristics, which are visible when baptized in the Father, Son and Holy Spirit.

The word baptism means different things to many people. Men like John G. Lake believed in repeated immersions. I believe Jesus meant this as well when He told His disciples to baptize in the names of the Godhead.

Philip, Paul and Peter were well acquainted with baptism and knew firsthand the importance and significance of being buried with Christ. One important point to make at this juncture is found in Acts 18:25 and 19:3–5

> *This man was instructed in the way of the Lord; and being fervent in the spirit, he spoke and taught diligently the things of the Lord, knowing only the baptism of John.*
>
> Acts 18:25

*And he said, into what then were ye baptized? And they said, Into John's baptism. And Paul said, John baptized with the baptism of repentance, saying unto the people that they **should believe on him** that should come after him, that is, **on Jesus**. And when they heard this, **they were baptized into the name of the Lord Jesus.***

ACTS 19: 3–5

Paul is clearly defining the difference between John's baptism and the one that immerses the participant "into" Christ. Baptism was also a point of contention among the early Church in Corinth, as Paul mentions in 1 Corinthians 1:10–17.

*Because it has come to my knowledge, through those of the house of Chloe, that there are **divisions among you**, my brothers. That is, that some of you say, I am of Paul; some say, I am of Apollos; some say, I am of Cephas; and some say, I am Christ's. **Is there a division in Christ?** was Paul nailed to the cross for you? or were you given **baptism in the name** of Paul? **For Christ sent me not to baptize, but to preach the gospel**: not in wisdom of words, lest the cross of Christ should be made void. For the word of the cross is to them that perish foolishness; but unto us who are saved it is the power of God.*

1 CORINTHIANS 1: 11–13, 17–18

Today, churches are wondering why there is no unity. However, they have never understood baptism into Christ and the power and declaration it makes in the heavens. **Immersion into Christ produces a substance, which forms your character.** Paul knew the power of true baptism, and so does the devil. The Father also knows, and at the river Jordan He spoke audibly in approval of His Son's action.

28

GODHEAD IMMERSION

Tenderness toward the lost and dying of this world is the result of baptism into the nature of the Father and exchanges our stony heart for one of flesh. The Father's heart is one of strength, power, dignity, love and giving without measure. A heart whose desire is to produce and reproduce after His kind and have dominion over all the forces that would steal, kill and destroy His precious children.

Baptism into the nature of the Son produces obedience to the Father. A Son whose only goal is to please the Father and establish His kingdom on earth as it is in heaven. Baptism into His nature and character reproduces a company of Sons prepared to rule and reign with the Lord Himself.

The immersion into the Holy Spirit baptizes us into the manifestations of the Godhead. In the Hebrew, Holy Spirit is translated Ruah Hakodesh, which is the feminine word from Kadosh, meaning holy. This is a picture of the tenderness of a Mother. The sweet, tender Holy Spirit whose love and compassion has sustained me and encouraged me on many occasions. In Genesis 1:2 we find that the precious Holy Spirit hovers or broods over the earth like a Mother, protecting and preparing the land for her children. The Holy Spirit endeavors to draw the children of God back to the Father in the same way that our earthly mothers protect and defend their families.

In essence, Jesus is commanding us to give up everything to be His disciples and enter the waters of baptism. The baptism Jesus is speaking of replaces our earthly family with the heavenly Godhead. The heavenly family of the Father, Son and Holy Spirit are the model for the Father, Son and Motherly operation of the Spirit. **The heavenly model replaces the family we renounce in Luke 14:26:**

> *If any man come to me, and hate not his father, and mother, and wife, and children, and brethren, and sisters, yea, and his own life also, he cannot be my disciple.*

29

The life of the real Christian should display the tri-une character of the Godhead in holiness, tenderness, love, creation, sacrifice and obedience. This nature will produce Christians trained to believe with the mind of Christ. The exchange of the earthly family for our heavenly one will force us to go beyond our soul and depend on our spirits.

I think it is important to be very clear about the results of the baptism we are discussing. Many churches teach about the struggle Christians will have with the "old man." In fact, some demonstrate this teaching by carrying a person on his back, representing the old man. Nothing is farther from the truth. Paul makes this point very clear in Romans 6.

> *So how can we still live under sin's influence?*
> *Don't you know that all of us who were baptized into Christ Jesus were baptized into his death? When we were baptized into his death, we were placed into the tomb with him. As Christ was brought back from death to life by the glorious power of the Father, so we, too, should live a new kind of life.*
> ***Being conscious that our old man was put to death** on the cross with him, so that the body of sin might be put away, and **we might no longer be servants to sin.** Even so see yourselves as dead to sin, but living to God in Christ Jesus.*
>
> Romans 6:2–4, 6, 11
> (Amplified)

Erroneous teaching is the result of a gospel not founded on the principles of discipleship and patterned after the life of Jesus. **Fulfilling all righteousness leaves no room for sin or failure.** Of course, all human beings make mistakes and sin.

Nevertheless, there is a big difference between sins of immaturity and those made from a consciousness of sin. The old man, is supposed to be dead, not strapped to our backs.

C. SANCTIFICATION IN THE WILDERNESS

After our baptism into the Godhead we will be led into the wilderness to begin working out our salvation, as Paul says in Philippians 2:12. The victory in the wilderness by Jesus is a strategic design to illustrate the power of sanctification and Christ consciousness.

> *My dear friends, you have always obeyed, not only when I was with you but even more now that I'm absent. In the same way **continue to work out your salvation with fear and trembling**.*
>
> PHILIPPIANS 2:12

The wilderness experience is fundamental in our transformation, particularly as it relates to transferring our belief center back to the spirit and forming the consciousness of Christ. **One of the greatest obstacles of our present age has been the implied message that great faith averts trials and tribulations. If this were the truth, why would the Holy Spirit lead Jesus into the wilderness?**

> *And when the tempter came to him, he said, if thou were the Son of God, command that these stones be made bread.*
> *But he answered and said, it is written, Man shall not live by bread alone, but by every word that proceeds out of the mouth of God.*

31

Then the devil takes him up into the holy city, and sets him on a pinnacle of the temple,
And said unto him, If thou be the Son of God, cast thyself down: for it is written, He shall give his angels charge concerning thee: and in their hands they shall bear thee up, lest at any time thou dash thy foot against a stone.
Jesus said unto him, it is written again, Thou shall not tempt the Lord thy God.
Again, the devil takes him up into an exceeding high mountain, and shows him all the kingdoms of the world, and the glory of them;
And said unto him, all these things will I give thee, if thou will fall down and worship me.
Then said Jesus unto him, get behind, Satan: for it is written, Thou shall worship the Lord thy God, and him only shall thou serve.
Then the devil left him, and, behold, angels came and ministered unto him.

MATTHEW 5–11

God used the devil in order to test the spirit, soul and body of Jesus.

For example, after forty days without food, the devil suggested that Jesus change the stone to bread in an effort to tempt His physical body. The temptation of the soul came in the form of calling on angels to rescue Him after jumping from a cliff. Finally, to test His spirit the devil vowed to give Him the kingdoms of this world for His worship

His spirit instead of His soul responded and defeated each temptation. Unlike Adam, Jesus refused to lose the dominion exercised by His spirit. **The word of God is spirit, and the devil is no match for God.** The devil knew Jesus spoke what He **believed. If we want to prevail against the enemy, our words must coincide with our behavior.**

If we are quoting scriptures such as, *"by His stripes we are healed,"* we should not be taking medications. If we are saying, *"No weapon formed against me shall prosper,"* we should not be buying home-security systems. We have seen the essential characteristics of a disciple and the power of baptism into the Godhead. Now we will enter into the next level: sanctification of truth.

D. SANCTIFIED BY THE TRUTH

> *Sanctify them in the truth; your word is truth.*
> *And for their sakes I sanctify myself, so that they also may be sanctified in truth.*
> *I ask not only on behalf of these, but also on behalf of those who will **believe** in me through their word, that they may all be one. As you, Father, are in me and I am in you, may they also be in us, so that the world may **believe** that you have sent me.*
> JOHN 17:17, 19–21

Believing as Jesus does requires sanctification in the truth. Truth is a person. God's word is truth. The word is Jesus. The word baptizes your mind. But the word is not separate from the person. Be baptized or washed in Jesus. Removing our character is possible only through immersion in the character of the Son. Our mind is disengaged. Our thinking is not the same any longer. Our only purpose is to reveal Jesus. **The truth is, you reveal outwardly what you inwardly believe.**

Jesus purified His spirit, soul and body in order to access the power of His Father. He knew that unless every part of His being was consecrated, the enemy could hinder His assignment. His mind must be as pure as His spirit.

33

Jesus was born the seed of Abraham, meaning his soul and body had to be formed in the likeness of His spirit. Therefore, He made ever-ascending steps back to the Father in order to demonstrate to all mankind the process and power of sanctification.

Jesus, the spotless Lamb of God, descends from heaven into man, in order for a sinless man to ascend back to the Father. Once Jesus stepped out of the river Jordan and the Holy Spirit descended upon Him, the process of sanctification had begun. The Holy Spirit orchestrated and directed each step in order for Jesus, the sinless Godman, to ascend back to His Father. The same process is available to you and me today because of Jesus and the Holy Spirit. **The same authority that Jesus used to destroy the works of the devil is available to us. Why? He has already stripped away the source of the enemies' power — namely, fear and unbelief**.

What about you? When you quote scripture, do you quote it from the position of believing in your spirit or from the knowledge in your mind? Perhaps you are not even sure of the difference between the two places. Before you finish this book, I pray the Holy Spirit will release wave after wave of fresh revelations into your life. Open your spirit wide to receive it right now.

Pray this prayer out loud: Holy Spirit I renounce the hidden things of my heart right now. I repent from every structure of unbelief and doubt concerning your words. I ask you to forgive me for not trusting you. I ask you to open my spirit to hear your voice and show me how to remove all the wrong systems of believing that have controlled my life. Jesus, please immerse me in your light and truth that we maybe one as You and Your Father are one.

Then Jesus went back full of and under the power of the Holy Spirit into Galilee.

So He came to Nazareth, where He had been brought up, and He entered the synagogue, as was His custom on the Sabbath day. And He stood up to read.

And there was handed to Him the book of the prophet Isaiah. He opened the book and found the place where it was written, **The Spirit of the Lord is upon Me, because He has anointed Me to preach the good news to the poor; He has sent Me to announce release to the captives and recovery of sight to the blind, to send forth as delivered those who are oppressed, who are downtrodden, bruised, crushed, and broken down by calamity, To proclaim the accepted and acceptable year of the Lord the day when salvation and the free favors of God profusely abound.** *Then He rolled up the book and gave it back to the attendant and sat down; and the eyes of all in the synagogue were gazing attentively at Him.*

And He began to speak to them: Today this Scripture has been fulfilled awhile you are present and hearing.

LUKE 4:14, 16–21
(AMPLIFIED)

Jesus returned in the power and control of the Holy Ghost to display in the flesh the prophecy of Isaiah 61. **The anointing described in this scripture is the consciousness of Christ. That anointing is available today to everyone who believes the same as Jesus.**

E. DEVELOPING HIS LIFE IN THE MIRACULOUS

It is important for us to observe the manner in which Jesus conquered nature, disease and death. Each healing or miracle He performed was on an ever-ascending scale of authority. Jesus was a student of His Father's laws and principles.

Therefore, He understood the dominion relinquished to the devil by the first Adam.

- **CONQUERING NATURE**

Jesus began His miraculous ministry by conquering nature in three ever-ascending levels. He changed water to wine. He stilled the raging seas while crossing the Galilee. Finally, He walked on the water. Each miracle was a step or ascent to the next level of miracles.

- **CREATIVE MIRACLES**

The next level of advancing His soul was the creative life of God. His feeding of the multitudes astounded His followers. He used the creative power of God in the area of multiplication. There is a distinction between healing and miracles. **Miracles are creative. Healing is restoring what has been lost.**

- **HEALING MIRACLES**

Jesus now advanced in the orders of sickness. When Jesus conquered nature, He did not need to overcome the free will and soul of a human being. **However, when He entered into healing, He had to dominate the sin consciousness of man. Jesus achieved this by revealing the heart of His Father to the minds and souls of the sick.** The result of that contact was love, for which nothing in hell can defeat.

The first person Jesus healed was Peter's mother-in-law. Jesus advanced in His healing anointing when He met and healed the blind man. Then finally He healed the lepers. **Each healing demonstrates the mastery of His soul by the Holy Spirit. Each order has degrees or levels of progression.**

Jesus advanced into the creative realm and formed eyes in a man born blind. This demonstration revealed a power in His consciousness that was preparing Him for His future goal of resurrection.

The power to perform miracles in our life will be directly proportionate to the amount of love for Jesus we truly possess. In other words, Jesus loved His Father more than His own life. That love became the catalyst by which faith reproduced the desires of the Father. Therefore, the more Jesus grew in His love for His Father, the more compassion He displayed for the ones His Father created.

In order for you or me to manifest miracles on earth today, we must be willing to give our life for Jesus. The power of His love will connect our faith with the desires of Christ to reproduce the kingdom of God on earth as it is in heaven. Beloved, if your spirit receives this one truth your struggles will be over. The miracle you have been asking God for was always waiting on your love for Him. The minute that issue is resolved, the miracle is yours. Jesus has been waiting on all of us to show Him how much we love Him. Words are not as important as actions, according to James. Therefore, it is imperative that we do the works of Jesus because that demonstrates the Father's heart.

• RESURRECTION MIRACLES

He now advanced in the authority over death. He began by raising Jairus' daughter, who had only been dead a few minutes. He passed by a funeral in Nain and commanded a boy who had been dead a few hours to awake. Then, although His friend Lazarus had been dead for four days, Jesus arrested the decomposing body and commanded him to come forth. Then Jesus announced His own death and resurrection by saying in John 10:18, *"I have the power to lay it down, and I have the power to take it again."*

F. JESUS MAKES THE SCRIPTURES HIS REALITY

Jesus searched out the promises of God in the scriptures and made them His by **believing.** This means that His promises to us are not made on speculation or supposition but because **His soul possessed the mind of God.**

Jesus would find in the scriptures the promises of supply and feeding the multitudes. He studied the creation of man from Genesis and formed eyes from clay for the blind. Jesus not only found the scriptures relating to supply but He also found the ones concerning His death and resurrection. **The key to His dominion was in His believing.** The words from His Father were not merely vocabulary but the very life or substance of His Father, imparted into every cell of His being.

Jesus had to become the spotless Lamb of God by sanctifying his body and soul. The consecration process required Him to become God's word in each cell of His being. He demonstrated the power of God's word to transform and conform His soul and body to His spirit. For example, He had to study the scriptures that spoke of the Christ in Deuteronomy 18:15, 17, Psalms 110:1 and Isaiah 9:6, to name a few. His spirit fed on the words of His Father to the prophets until every part of His being was transformed into the Christ.

Once He purified His total being, His Father and He are One. Now He and His Father become the words they speak. That understanding will give us insight into the blueprint for believing.

Jesus was one with His Father. That statement rolls off our tongues as if it were an easy task to perform. **But it was not easy. The devil has blinded us with religion, making us believe the temptations of this world were effortless for Jesus**. If this is your belief, you may need to reread scriptures in Hebrews 4:15–16, 5:8–9 describing that, as High Priest, He was tempted like we are, and even though He was a Son, He had to suffer to become the author of eternal salvation.

*If you live in me and what I say **lives in you**, then ask for anything you want, and it will be yours.*

JOHN 15:7

The scripture in John 15:7 begins with the word **If.** The responsibility is ours just as it was Jesus. The same way Jesus searched out the word for His identity is our design to obtain the mind of Christ. Jesus said, **"All things are possible if we can believe" (Mark 9:23).** The question is, do we believe from inside Him or outside? Are we speaking His words or our thoughts?

> *Do you not believe that I am in the Father, and that the Father is in Me? What I am telling you I do not say on My own authority and of My own accord; but the Father Who lives continually in Me does the works. Believe Me that I am in the Father and the Father in Me; or else believe Me for the sake of the very works themselves. If you cannot trust Me, at least let these works that I do in My Father's name convince you. I assure you, most solemnly I tell you, if anyone stead-fastly believes in Me, he will himself be able to do the things that I do; and he will do even greater things than these, because I go to the Father.*
>
> JOHN 14:10–12 (AMPLIFIED)

Before the creation of the universe Jesus knew His assignment, therefore, as He studied the scriptures He became conscious of that decision. His assignment was to redeem and empower Sons with kingdom authority. **Once we reside in Jesus, we will become conscious of our assignment and responsibility we accepted. That is the Christ consciousness, which will bring the love and power to overcome this life. Can you see it?**

3. DEALING WITH OUR UNBELIEF

The lack of power and anointing is our own fault. Jesus has shown us how to be overcomers. Unfortunately, the unwillingness to believe Jesus has restricted us to a life that struggles with skepticism. Unbelief and doubt are sadly the norm in most Christians. **However, if we are willing to pay the price for the mind of Christ, dominion and supernatural living will be the result**.

The following scripture demonstrates to perfection the Christ consciousness and the Church today.

> *Rabbi, answered one of the crowd, I have brought you my son.* He has a dumb spirit in him; and wherever it comes upon him, it dashes him to the ground, and he foams at the mouth and grinds his teeth, and he is pining away. I begged your disciples to expel it, but they had not the power. **O unbelieving generation!** *Replied Jesus; how long must I be with you? How long must I have patience with you? Bring the boy to me.*
>
> *So they brought him to Jesus. And the spirit, when he saw Jesus, immediately threw the youth into convulsions, so that he fell on the ground and rolled about, foaming at the mouth.*
>
> *Then Jesus asked the father,* **how long has he been like this?** *From early childhood, he said; and often it has thrown him into the fire or into pools of water to destroy him.* **But, if you possibly can,** *have pity on us and help us.*
>
> **If I possibly can!** *Replied Jesus;* **why, everything is possible to him who believes.**
>
> *Immediately the father cried out,* **I believe: help my unbelief.**
>
> *Then Jesus, seeing that an increasing crowd was running towards Him, rebuked the foul spirit, and said to it, Dumb and deaf spirit, I command you, come out of him and never enter into him again.*
>
> *So with a loud cry he threw the boy into fit after fit, and came out. The boy looked as if he were dead, so that*

*most of them said he was dead; but Jesus took his hand
and raised him up, and he stood on his feet.*

MARK 9:17–27

Jesus returns from the mount of transfiguration to a tumult
among His disciples, who were unable to deliver a boy with a
deaf and dumb spirit. The transcendent glory Jesus had just
experienced most certainly remained in some portion of His
body and clothing. Immediately upon arriving, He was met
with doubt and unbelief.

I can remember being interrupted by a phone call while
experiencing a powerful presence of God. The person on the
other end of the phone was hysterical. She was convinced her
son was going to die because of the doctor's report. I asked her,
"why she chose to believe the doctor instead of God's Word?"

Many times our wrong reaction to bad news is the
entrance the enemy uses to bring doubt and unbelief. One
lesson I have learned over the years is to listen to the Holy
Spirit more attentively than I listen to others, especially when
entering a hospital or setting where the environment is more
likely to contain doubt and unbelief. I am not saying to be
rude or unresponsive to people, but make sure you are hearing the truth from the Lord instead of reports from persons
who are hysterical. *You will recall how Jesus would remove those
He perceived would hinder His belief* (Mark 5:40).

Jesus was obviously disturbed by the unbelief and rebuked
them by saying, "unbelieving generation," or as one translation says, "generation without faith."

Regrettably, many times, because of unbelief, sickness and
disease are rampant in the churches. The attitude among most
Christian pastors and leaders is to wait on the famous Christian
healers and evangelists to address their troubles. This is exactly
what Jesus was rebuking. We as Christians should not wait on
anyone to heal the sick, cast out demons and raise the dead.
This is what the Bible says in Mark 16:16–18:

*He who **believes** and is baptized shall be saved, but he who disbelieves will be condemned. And signs shall attend those who **believe**, even such as these. By making use of my name they shall expel demons. They shall speak new languages. They shall take up venomous snakes, and if they drink any deadly poison it shall do them no harm whatever. They shall lay their hands on the sick, and the sick shall recover.*

Brothers and Sisters if you believe, why would you need anyone else to do what you have been equipped to handle?

In the story with the demonized child, Jesus called the father to bring his son to Him. Immediately the demon put on a show to steal the attention and terrify everyone. Jesus quickly recaptured the mind of the father by asking a question. "How long has your son been possessed?" **Jesus was not concerned with the answer. He wanted the father to stop focusing on the devil and open his spirit to believe in the supernatural**.

The father finally asked Jesus to have pity and help him. Sadly, many Christians who are crying to God for their healing have the same attitude: "Jesus have pity on me." Beloved, Jesus has given *you* the authority and power over every evil thing on the earth. *"All things are possible to those who believe."* **The reality is that the Church, for the most part, does not believe**. Oh, we are familiar with all the stories of the great miracles. **Nevertheless, making the transition from our minds to our spirits where faith resides seems impossible.**

The reaction by the father is the sobering reality of the Church today. And straightway the father of the child cried out, and said with tears, Lord, I believe; help thou mine unbelief.

The truth is, belief and unbelief cannot coexist. Unbelief corrupts belief. We either believe or we do not, and judging by the numbers of sick and diseased in the Church, it is easy to see which is the case. Dearly beloved, this ought not to be.

We must follow the pattern of Christ, in order to believe the way He does. **The consciousness of Christ is the power to believe in the supernatural. The mind of Christ is the spirit and soul of man united in faith and believing.**

How can you know if you believe from your spirit? Signs and wonders will be the result. Jesus studied the scriptures until His spirit connected with the Holy Ghost. The result is the miraculous.

Study the scriptures the same way. Ask the Holy Ghost to reveal, by His mercy, revelation and truth what is preventing you from entering into Him? He will, and once He does, you will repent. **The reason why is because you have never believed?** Repenting is not a light thing. Just like the father in the story above, you must cry out and recognize your unbelief.

The same way that Jesus had mercy on the father, who recognized his unbelief, is the way to receive help now. **Begin in truth and repentance and experience your faith growing supernaturally to believe in all things.**

Chapter Three

Believing is the Substance of our Reality

1. WHAT IS SUBSTANCE?

*Now faith is the **substance** of things hoped for, the evidence of things not seen.*

HEBREWS 11:1

By faith we understand that the worlds were prepared by the word of God, so that what is seen was not made out of things which are visible.

HEBREWS 11:3

The physical world was created from the invisible. The Bible says God called things that were not into being.

Abraham believed when he stood in the presence of the God who gives life to dead people and calls into existence nations that don't even exist.

ROMANS 4:17

The invisible world has shape, even though it is hard to describe. Perhaps fire, light or spirit is the best way to portray the heavenly substance.

When Christ touches us for the first time by the heavenly substance of the Holy Spirit, we will at once sense a void inside our beings. **Emptiness creates a longing for stability, which requires a belief system. In general, the substances or materials of the fallen nature of man created the systems of this world. Therefore, man puts his trust and faith in these systems with predictable consequences consistent with sin, sickness and death.** Man believes he is making correct decisions and wise choices in the best interest of society, but the reality will be disaster. Consequently, what he thinks is good is truly evil.

In order to understand the "substance" our belief is made from, we should understand the definitions.

Substance means: *whether material or spiritual; that which is real,* in distinction from that which is apparent; real or existing essence; *the most important element in any existence; the characteristic and essential components of anything.*

Throughout our study we will discuss different types of substances.

2. SUBSTANCES OF HEAVEN

We are filled with the substance of heaven in the measure we know the Lord. Jesus best reveals it in the following scripture.

> *Not everyone who says to me, Lord, Lord, will enter the kingdom of heaven, but only the one who does the will of my Father in heaven.*
> *On that day many will say to me, Lord, Lord, did we not prophesy in your name, and cast out*

demons in your name, and do many deeds of power in your name?

*Then I will declare to them, **I never knew you**; go away from me, you evildoers.*

Everyone then who hears these words of mine and acts on them will be like a wise man that built his house on rock.

The rain fell, the floods came, and the winds blew and beat on that house, but it did not fall, because it had been founded on rock.

And everyone who hears these words of mine and does not act on them will be like a foolish man who built his house on sand.

The rain fell, and the floods came, and the winds blew and beat against that house, and it fell—and great was its fall!

MATTHEW 7:21–27

Jesus says, in essence, *knowing me* is more than prophesying and casting out demons. The word used to describe a man and woman intimately loving one another is **know**. Women can be married to wealthy men with privileges to purchase expense gifts without having an intimate relationship with their husband. This is a selfish relationship without responsibility. **Responsibility will demand love and intimacy in any relationship. This is lawless in the eyes of God and is, sadly, the condition of many people who call themselves Christians**.

Many have entered a selfish relationship with the Lord. Moreover, the lack of relationship makes it easy for them to be irresponsible as well. Because of this, their Christianity lacks real substance. Let us read the story of the man who sowed seeds in Mark 4.

A man went out to put seed in the earth:
And while he was doing it, some was dropped by the wayside, and the birds came and took it for food.

47

> *And some went on the stones, where it had not much*
> *earth; and it came up straight away, because the earth*
> *was not deep:*
> *And when the sun was high, it was burned; and because*
> *it had no root, it became dry and dead.*
> *And some went among the thorns, and the thorns came*
> *up, and it had no room for growth and gave no fruit.*
> *And some, falling on good earth, gave fruit, coming up*
> *and increasing, and giving thirty, sixty, and a hundred*
> *times as much.*
>
> MARK 4:3–8

The seed is Jesus and His consciousness. The depth of who He is and everything He has already accomplished is the eternal revelation that will unfold for the ages to come.

The least of His profound accomplishments is salvation. The soil is the condition of our hearts where believing must begin. The impediments, such as **rocks** and **thorns**, are the **substances** inside our souls preventing us from becoming His disciples and accepting the responsibility for humanity. **The hearts of those who have consecrated themselves are bearing fruit according to the level of their sanctification in their spirit, soul and bodies**.

The story found in Luke 6:47–49 describe two foundations upon which to build a house.

> *I will show you what someone is like who comes to me,*
> *hears my words, and acts on them.*
> *That one is like a man building a house, **who dug***
> ***deeply and laid the foundation on rock;** when a*
> *flood arose, the river burst against that house but could*
> *not shake it, because it had been well built.*
> *But the one who hears and does not act is like a man*
> *who built a house on the ground without a foundation.*

When the river burst against it, immediately it fell, and
great was the ruin of that house.

LUKE 6:47–49

**The depth of our foundation in Christ is visible through
our sacrifice, commitment and consecration.** We may encounter humiliation, suffering, hardships and most certainly discomfort. **However, unless we are willing to trust the Holy
Ghost in our renovations, our structure will not endure.**
Moreover, we will not produce fruit for the kingdom of God.
Oh yes, **we may cast out a few devils and prophesy, but entering the kingdom requires foundation and fruit production.**

The rock of course is Jesus Christ. The foundation is our
consciousness or belief systems. **The Spirit and Consciousness
of Christ is the substance upon which our belief rests. This
is much more than just His word; His actual substance must
enter into our hearts and minds.**

We have defined substance as that which underlies all outward manifestations. **Therefore, our actions reveal the invisible foundation that constructs our beliefs.**

In other words, substance is the matter or material that
shapes a belief system. Remember, our definition for **belief
system describes a structure of believing, which may or may
not be true and produces a behavior constructed from information or substances either visible or invisible.**

For example, the Wright Brothers believed that man could
fly. The airplane was the visible evidence of their imaginations
and became substance, and this substance gave birth to their
creation.

In order to examine substance in detail, let us imagine
what may have happened to the Wright brothers, who invented
the airplane.

The Bible says in James 1:17 that every good and perfect
gift is from heaven. Many people probably dreamed of flying;

49

after all, the laws of aerodynamics were the same at creation as in the twentieth century. Nevertheless, no one created a flying machine until the Wright brothers.

Their dream became an inspiration, and the Holy Spirit released a substance into their spirits. Faith is the invisible substance in Hebrews 11:1. We will learn later the **invisible substance we call faith is actually Jesus.**

Faith in the hearts of these men became knowledge in their souls. Nevertheless, it was not until these men **believed in the invisible substance** of their inspirations and dreams that it became a reality.

One important point to see in this illustration is that the invisible substance became a blueprint for reality. **The invisible becomes visible as faith becomes tangible.** Many creative people say, "if I can see it in my mind, I can produce it in the natural world."

Many people **believe** they will get sick during each year; this produces a negative **substance** that manifests as infection and disease, and the **reality** results in a visit to a physician. What is the substance of our foundation, rock or sand?

3. SUBSTANCE EQUALS WEALTH

Most of us believe a professional career in medicine, engineering or computer sciences is necessary in order to obtain material wealth. Therefore, we are encouraged to study hard in schools to achieve the highest possible academic achievements. However, we have determined in this discussion that the invisible created the visible. **So why is it that we spend more time pursuing the visible rather than the invisible?**

A person's wealth or material goods are also his substance. One of the many remarkable scriptures in the Bible is Matthew 4:18–22:

*As he was walking along the Sea of Galilee, he saw two brothers, Simon (called Peter) and Andrew. They were throwing a net into the sea because they were fishermen. Jesus said to them, Come, follow me! I will teach you how to catch people instead of fish. They **immediately left their nets and followed him**.*
*As Jesus went on, he saw two other brothers, James and John, the sons of Zebedee. They were in a boat with their father Zebedee preparing their nets to go fishing. He called them, and they **immediately left the boat and their father and followed Jesus**.*

Those who follow Jesus are blessed, but those who leave everything are true disciples. Many times people will follow Jesus after they have lost everything and have nothing left to lose, but those four brothers left their jobs, family and security to follow Jesus. In reality, **they left their substance for a belief. In other words, their belief in Jesus caused them to leave a tangible resource for an invisible supply.**

This is not to say that education, knowledge and pursuing your interest are unfruitful. On the contrary, the mind is an extraordinary instrument designed to construct and implement systems beneficial to the kingdom of God. **However, the belief systems of this world, which are the foundation of most educational systems, will not educate anyone about the kingdom of God**.

If we spent more time alone with the Holy Spirit, meditating on the words of Jesus, our capacity to believe would unite with our spirits, producing dramatic results. **One outcome would be our spirits and souls connected to our faith with believing. The power of this connection is the consciousness we have been discussing**.

One day I was praying for a woman who had cancer. Before I could touch this person, the Holy Spirit said, "wait."

I stepped back and just listened. All of a sudden, I sensed something coming into my body that felt like electricity. Then the Holy Spirit said, "Release this sensation into this person now." When I touched the person, a burst, like lightning, shot through my body into hers. She fell onto the floor. While she lay there, I saw the Holy Spirit healing her.

I received a call the following month of her healing from the pastor of the woman's church. The substance of God passed through my body and dissolved the cancer. This is an example of believing with the Spirit. Praise His holy name.

The more we uncover the truth about believing the better we will understand our substance. **Substance is our physical and spiritual composition or structure. Believing creates a structure built by information, hearsay, rumor, innuendo and a myriad of other thoughts and impressions.**

Are you beginning to see the relationship between who and what you are in relationship to your beliefs? **If we follow a logical progression, we will conclude our insides and outsides or substance will resemble that which we believe.**

Throughout our entire discussion, continue to ask the Holy Spirit to reveal to your spirits more revelation. This exercise will train your spirit to become the authority in your life. You will be amazed at how quickly your surroundings will change.

TANGIBLE VERSUS INTANGIBLE

Most of us have heard the messages of faith over the years. They are very essential and significant for anyone who follows Christ. Perhaps one of the most quoted scriptures regarding faith is in Hebrews 11:1 (several different translations following).

> *Now faith is the substance of things hoped for, the evidence of things not seen.*
> NEW KING JAMES VERSION

Now faith is a well-grounded assurance of that for which we hope, and a conviction of the reality of things, which we do not see.

WEYMOUTH

Faith assures us of things we expect and convinces us of the existence of things we cannot see.

GOD'S WORD

One resounding truth, which emanates from this scripture, is the inseparable connection between the invisible and visible. **Faith is to the spirit of man what believing is in the soul.** You may be thinking, "But wait a minute; you said the reason for all of our troubles is because we believe from our souls." Absolutely, and I will explain why.

Man is a spirit, with a soul and body. Adam had the ability to see the visible and the invisible at any time. The Bible says, *"God walked with man in the cool of the evening,"* which seems to indicate Adam's ability to see both the spiritual and physical realm, since God is Spirit. The fall removed man from one of the purposes of God, which was to commune with Him face to face in the spirit.

Faith is a spiritual material or substance of God. **The Holy Spirit releases this substance according to the demand made on Him by someone's spirit and soul**. This demand is what many people call "releasing" our faith.

For example, when Jesus resurrected Lazarus, His spirit and soul released the invisible faith and produced the visible miracle. Miracles encourage people to believe. Christians must allow their spirits to dominate their believing if they want to live in the supernatural.

Jesus trained His soul to believe according to His spirit. That was the location of the Words of His Father. This should be the first goal of every Christian. Otherwise, how can you trust the Bible? The Bible is spirit.

53

The substance of the Bible is the invisible God mani-fested in words. Herein lies the heart of our current discussion. The invisible realm is the source of the substance or material matter. Most Bible teachers describe the invisible substance as faith. In our description of the invention of the airplane, faith was the substance from the invisible made visible in a flying machine.

One of the questions asked most often by Christians is why is my faith not working. My response to this question is found in Habakkuk 2:4.

Behold, he that is unbelieving, his soul shall not be right in himself: but the just shall live in his faith.

The truth is, many Christians who ask that question are more interested in material substance than spiritual. This is not a condemnation because the distinctions between the soul and spirit are misunderstood.

Tribulations forced me to study the scriptures to under-stand why my faith was not working. Many of the truths from that search are in this book. **One truth that helped me and will help you is the revelation of Christ. That understanding alone transformed my doubt and unbelief, and it will do the same for you.**

LUKEWARM

4. CHRIST IS KNOCKING AT THE DOOR

We have the opportunity to travel to many places in the world. The love we experience by the mercy of the Lord in addition to the opportunity to minister to so many all over the world truly humbles me. My heart rejoices each time I look into the eyes of God's children and see the hunger for, and expectation of, experiencing Jesus in deeper ways.

We hear so many miraculous stories of healings, deliverances and restoration that refresh and build our faith. One story involved a woman whose life was in chaos. Her husband had left her, and her daughter died in an automobile accident. She was devastated. We had the opportunity to minister to her and bring her prophetic guidance from the Holy Spirit. The next year when we returned, her life had completely changed. She had been given a large amount of land, which she used to shelter unwed mothers and runaway children. The Lord used her to rescue hundreds of women and change their lives. The government of that country supported her efforts with money and tax exempt status. The Lord restored her and gave her many daughters to replace the pain of losing her own.

Stories like that are common among people who come to the Lord and believe Him for their very existence.

Sadly, when we return to the United States and listen to many Christians we do not hear the same excitement, testimonies and hunger in their voices. Of course, we do hear stories of miracles, but not to the extent as in other countries. Is it because God is not visiting the United States? The answer to that is a resounding **No**. The Lord is desperate for this country to return to their covenant with Him. One problem preventing many of the people of the United States from a fresh experience with the Holy Ghost is **their wrong belief. The crowds and prosperity convince them that what they are doing is right in the eyes of God.**

I have asked the Holy Ghost the reason for this condition, and the only word the Holy Ghost said was "Laodicea." There have been many sermons and books written on that church described by Jesus in Revelation 3:14–22.

The truth is the Laodicea spirit afflicts us all in the Western world. **This spirit is one, of the seven anti-Christ spirits released against the Church**. A complete study of the other churches Jesus describes in Chapters 2 and 3 of Revelation is critical for understanding the spiritual principalities. Nevertheless, for the purposes of our study, let us examine 3:18–20.

> *If you are wise you will get from me gold tested by fire, so that you may have true wealth; and white robes to put on, so that your shame may not be seen; and oil for your eyes, so that you may see. I rebuke and discipline as many as I love; be zealous therefore and repent.*
>
> *See, I am waiting at the door and giving the sign; if my voice comes to any man's ears and he makes the door open, I will come in to him, and will take food with him and he with me.*
>
> REVELATION 3:18–20

Jesus is explaining the solution to man's passion for wealth and wisdom, which originated in the Garden. In essence, **Jesus is saying that the substance of the Holy Spirit mixed with the substance of man's spirit produces true wealth. Gold tested by fire is the visible material formed from the mixture.**

> *I baptize you with water so that you will change the way you think and act. But the one who comes after me is more powerful than I. I am not worthy to remove his sandals. He will baptize you with the Holy Spirit and fire.*
>
> MATTHEW 3:11 (AMPLIFIED)

We have discussed at length the importance of baptism into the Godhead. However, this scripture reveals a level of immersion we must understand. Many people speak of baptism in the Spirit. The experience is very real and Biblical.

Many people believe and even say that speaking in tongues is the evidence of being "filled" with the Holy Spirit. Nothing can be further from the truth. Speaking in

an unknown tongue is a gift. First, if someone uses the word **filled** it implies full, with no room remaining.

Unfortunately, we have heard pastors describe people in their congregations as filled with the spirit because they speak in tongues. However, some of these same people also surf the Web for pornography and commit adultery. **Now, is it possible for someone filled to capacity with the Holy Spirit to sin?** Of course, the answer is no. This belief has created horrible consequences, the least of which is cheapening the experience with the precious Holy Spirit.

The truth is, the sweet Holy Spirit is searching for a sanctified vessel in which to reside. His purpose for leading Jesus into the wilderness was to complete His total consecration that He began at the river Jordan. **Is it reasonable for us to believe we can respond to an altar call, recite a sinner's prayer and have someone lay hands on us to be "filled" with the Holy Spirit without being consecrated as Jesus?**

The infilling begins on our crucifixion day, when our sinful nature is nailed on the cross finally. The resurrection was real in Jesus, and it will be for those who crucify their flesh with all its passions and desires. **These are the steps necessary for a vessel to house His personality and presence.** He does not take up residence in anyone who has not cleaned his vessel and moved to the servant's quarters. **Speaking with tongues is a tool that the Lord will give to any who ask, as an aid in cleaning the vessel for His occupation. Look at the additional promise of Jesus.**

> *Jesus answered him; Those who love me will do what I say. My Father will love them, and we will go to them and make our home with them*
>
> JOHN 14:23

The importance of the baptism in the Holy Spirit cannot be emphasized enough. **Do not stop until He possesses you. The Holy Spirit is the substance that produces the right believing and ultimately the true reality.** Do you understand?

Substance is the well or source from which right believing originates. If your substance is not He, the Holy Spirit, your believing and your reality will be false.

Further study of the Church at Laodicea uncovers the priceless rewards to those who leave.

> *...and white robes to put on, so that your shame may not be seen; and oil for your eyes, so that you may see.*
> REVELATION 3:18

Adam's awareness of his and Eve's nakedness was the reality of their sin and shame. Jesus gives the white robes and anointing oil as material substances for the heavenly substances of righteousness and revelation.

Many of the messages preached in the Western world appeal to the souls of man. Prosperity, health and emotional well-being are non-confrontational messages of peace, love and success. However, what types of defense will this offer against witchcraft and the occult? The devil has released blockbuster motion pictures that have captured the youth with the occult, such as the *Harry Potter* and *Lord of the Rings* series, to name just a couple. As a result, **deliverance** will be a word that the Church will become more familiar with in the next several years.

The devil is seeking those whom he may devour, and those whose belief and faith are on material substances are easy targets. The truth is that most of our problems lie with our own failure to study the scriptures for ourselves. We have been trained to rely on pastors for our spiritual needs, and many pastors are overwhelmed with churches whose congregations resemble Revelation 2 and 3.

I rebuke and discipline as many as I love; be zealous therefore and repent.

REVELATION 3:19

The Bible says to repent and embrace the chastisement of the Lord; instead, we believe primarily the messages, which promise comfort and prosperity. Our souls are delighted with luxury and pampering but revolt at the thought of discomfort and change. **The first line of defense against change is unbelief.**

Consequently, the Holy Spirit is sending prophets with messages, designed to challenge our comfort and believing. These messages are the product of the Father's love for His church. However, the devil has caused some people to believe that the more material substance they have, the more faith they possess.

There are many manifestations around the world today. In some places, we have seen gold appearing on people. In other places, we have heard of diamonds and precious stones manifesting. There are even reports of manna appearing. This may be the spiritual substance of the people manifesting the character and nature of Christ. Those whom I have met with these manifestations are beautiful Christians who love the Lord with all their hearts.

Manifestations, like miracles, are a way for the Lord to awake the soul from its mediocrity to the awesomeness of God. The danger in some cases is that man's soul becomes lazy and bored if not entertained with increasingly spectacular demonstrations of the supernatural.

I remember earnestly desiring the gold manifestation in my life. The truth was, this phenomenon would exalt me and make me appear "super" spiritual. **I am certainly not saying that this is the desire of those who are having these manifestations in their lives. I am only speaking about myself.**

After the Holy Ghost showed me how pitiful and immature it was for me to pursue signs instead of Him, I wept. **The material substance of the Holy Ghost I thought was inside me was just more of me**. My spirit wanted to glorify God but my soul's ambitions were impure and unholy. **The substance of this world will not produce holiness unless sanctified by the Holy Ghost.**

Dearly beloved, examine your substance today. Does it contain more of Him or more of you? The simplest way to answer that question is to ask the following. Of whose voice am I most conscious? Whose voice is the louder, the Holy Ghost's or mine?

Self-exaltation and more pleasure are the voices of self. The voice from the Spirit typically challenges the status quo and often requires sacrifice and discomfort. **The voice of the Spirit is not demanding but trustworthy. The voice of the Spirit is simple yet profound**. The voice of the Spirit will always resonate with the vibration of love, righteousness, peace and joy.

The more we hear the voice of the Holy Ghost the more of His substance remains. So if your body is manifesting gold because of the sanctification process of the Holy Ghost, hallelujah. **Never be satisfied with periodic manifestations of His presence. Do not be content until you raise the dead and the lame walk. In addition, the substance from your soul causes divine health in your own body.** If I could impart one thing to your spirit, it would be never to allow doubt or unbelief to enter your thoughts.

The substance you are currently can be changed by the one who created all things. **The one you trust is the source of your substance. If you are not satisfied with your condition, change the foundation of your belief.**

The substance of Christ is the authority over the natural laws in the following scripture.

But while they yet did not believe for joy, and were won-
dering, he said to them, Have ye anything here to eat?
And they gave him part of a broiled fish and of a hon-
eycomb; and he took it and ate before them. And he said
to them, These are the words that I spoke to you while
I was yet with you, that all that is written concerning
me in the Law of Moses and prophets and psalms must
be fulfilled.
Then he opened their understanding to understand the
scriptures, and said to them, Thus it is written, and
thus it behooved the Christ to suffer, and to rise from
among the dead the third day; and that repentance and
remission of sins should be preached in his name to all
the nations beginning at Jerusalem.
And ye are witnesses of these things.
And behold, I send the promise of my Father upon you;
but do ye remain in the city till ye be clothed with power
from on high.
And he led them out as far as Bethany, and having lifted
up his hands, he blessed them.
And it came to pass as he was blessing them; he was
separated from them and was carried up into heaven.
Luke 24:41–51

This amazing account of Jesus illustrates how little we understand the spirit realm. Jesus ascends into heaven from Bethany after He and His disciples eat fish. What happened to the fish in His stomach?

Obviously, spiritual laws surpass the natural laws we so quickly believe. The example above of material substance made invisible is dramatic. The laws of this world will submit to those whose spiritual substance is the same as Jesus. Therefore, if our substance is Jesus, everything else will

submit. That means every disease by any name must bow to the substance of Jesus. That means every resource needed to supply a need must submit to the substance of Jesus.

Jesus told His disciples in John 15:16 that *"whatever you ask the Father in my name He will give it to you."*

> *...till now ye did ask nothing in my name; ask, and ye shall receive, that your joy may be full.*
>
> JOHN 16:24

We will learn later that joy is a spiritual force designed for our bodies. The substance of Jesus is joy, peace and righteousness in the Holy Ghost.

Chapter Four

The Kingdom of God Transforms our Reality

1. UNDERSTANDING REALITY

Our next subject is your breakthrough, if you allow the Holy Spirit to change your failures into victory. We have progressed in our discussion to the understanding that whom, what and why we believe are rooted in the **substance** in which we trust. Our consciousness will operate as the first Adam if we do not surrender to the Holy Spirit. In other words, unless we have the mind of Christ, we will not believe as He does.

The reality we are living is the manifestation of whom and what we believe. Most of us have an idea of reality but for the sake of continuity let us look at some definitions.

Reality is: *that which exists; objectively all of your experiences that determine how things appear to you; the totality of all things possessing actuality, existence or essence.*

The sum total of our experiences shapes our reality. For example, since Biblical times, the Middle East has been a place of hostilities between the Arab and Jew. Generation after generation in both cultures have experienced tragedy in one form or another. These events and experiences have produced a reality of hatred and mistrust in their souls.

However, someone who is neither Jew nor Arab who observes the conflict may have a different reality. These people are objective because their experiences are not biased or prejudiced.

Another example of reality is that of church denominations. Research indicates as many as thirty thousand Protestant denominations worldwide without including the Eastern and Catholic religions. This is an astounding number. Members of these diverse denominations normally submit to a different doctrine or belief system.

In other words, one denomination may determine that healing, casting out demons and speaking in tongues is not relevant today, while other denominations will oppose this doctrine and establish another set of beliefs. Each denomination usually has very different interpretations of the Bible and God.

Many times the denomination believes more in its doctrine than the words of Christ and aspires to convince its members to believe accordingly. **Therefore, each of these denominations has defined its reality according to its beliefs.**

All religions are man's attempt to find the kingdom of God, which he lost at creation. Therefore, man creates religions and denominations as a mechanism for control and security. Man will surrender his control and a limited amount of his time to a system, which promises heaven. It is limited, because if it interferes with his money and time he will find an alternative. **Man is generally secure when he follows a religious dogma because of the belief that there is safety among the multitudes doing the same thing.** This religious activity allows people to follow a doctrine on Sunday and pursue their real ambitions the rest of the week. This is the attitude of millions of church-attending people.

Consequently, many of the larger churches in Western society are the ones whose goals appear to be non-confrontational and socially acceptable, and offer the promise of prosperity to their followers. Non-confrontational messages are popular because the pastors do not want to lose parishioners.

2. KINGDOM TRANSFORMATION PRINCIPLES

Jesus met the same type of reality in his time as we do now. His greatest battles were with the religious spirits. These spirits flourish in environments with rules and doctrines. Those spirits' purpose is to harden the hearts of those they possess. The problem is, those persons with these spirits are blinded and unable to see their condition.

Our ministry is one of hundreds throughout the earth whose goal is to establish the kingdom of God. The confrontation today is the same as in the time of Jesus.

And Jesus went about all Galilee, teaching in their synagogues, and preaching the gospel of the kingdom, and healing all manner of sickness and all manner of disease among the people.

MATTHEW 4:23

In my opinion, if our desire is to change society the way Jesus did we should follow His example. The method Jesus used was teaching the principles of God in the synagogues and preaching the kingdom of God to society. You may ask why I am saying principles and not doctrine.

For even though by this time you ought to be teaching others, you actually need someone to teach you over again the very first principles of God's Word. You have come to need milk, not solid food.

HEBREWS 5:12

Therefore leaving the principles of the doctrine of Christ, let us go on unto perfection.

HEBREWS 6:1

Principles are more important than doctrine because they establish Christ as the foundation. In order to know the principles of Jesus we must begin with Matthew.

> *He proceeded to teach them, and said: Blessed are those who recognize they are spiritually helpless the kingdom of heaven belongs to them.*
> *Blessed are the mourners, for they shall be comforted.*
> *Blessed are the meek, for they, as heirs shall obtain possession of the earth. Blessed are those who hunger and thirst for righteousness, for they shall be completely satisfied.*
> *Blessed are the compassionate, for they shall receive compassion.*
> *Blessed are the pure in heart, for they shall see God.*
> *Blessed are the peacemakers, for it is they who will be recognized as sons of God.*
> *Blessed are those who have borne persecution in the cause of Righteousness, for to them belongs the kingdom of the Heavens.*
> *Blessed are you when they have insulted and persecuted you, and have said every cruel thing about you falsely for my sake.*
>
> MATTHEW 5:2–11

Beloved, Jesus Christ the cornerstone is set upon this foundation. Every departure from these principles has divided the Church into denominations and robbed from us our daily bread. Practicing the truths of these verses will answer the questions we so desperately seek from God. **The simple return to these principles will unlock the supply of heaven and establish the foundation to build His kingdom.**

This is the plumb line by which we are all measured to determine how much of ourselves remain. If your spirit conforms to the principles of Christ, then your fruit will surely remain.

In my opinion, if the Body of Christ taught nothing but the principles found in Matthew 5, 6 and 7, the Holy Ghost would revisit us with signs and wonders of Biblical proportion. After Jesus taught the principles of His Father's kingdom, powerful demonstrations of the kingdom would manifest in the form of miracles. Society observed first-hand the principles of the kingdom and the transformed lives. The experiences produced a **reality** in the transformed **believers**, who then converted others from the **substance** inside their spirits. Do you see it? **Transformation occurs not only by word but also by the power of the Holy Ghost entering our spirits and producing a new reality.**

The time is fulfilled, and the **kingdom of God** *is at hand: repent ye, and* **believe the gospel.**

MARK 1:15

The kingdom of God had come in the flesh and the only way to enter was through Him, by repenting from the sin consciousness of believing the lie and **believing** the truth or the person Jesus.

The kingdom message is not to believe this doctrine or that creed or anything else. Only believe Jesus, His character, nature and principles. Jesus is the kingdom. The principles you exhibit confirm the kingdom to which you belong.

There is a kingdom of this world, which also has principles. It also has a king and his name is (little s on purpose) satan. Today as in the Garden of Eden, the same strategies are used. The goal of the devil is to maintain the veil over the eyes of man. The more man operates in darkness, the easier it is for the devil to use illusion and fear to control the soul. **A mind whose soul is in darkness is unaware of another kingdom and belief system.**

3. TRANSFORMED FROM WITHIN

A. SPIRIT, SOUL AND BODY SANCTIFICATION

The purpose of our reality as believers must penetrate beyond the peripheral and infiltrate every area of our being. Otherwise, the attraction of this world's kingdom will be overwhelming.

Our belief must produce the substance of Christ and the reality of His kingdom in every cell of our spirit, soul and body.

> *And the very God of peace sanctify you wholly; and I pray God your whole spirit and soul and body be preserved blameless unto the coming of our Lord Jesus Christ.*
>
> 1 THESSALONIANS 5:23

The early Church understood and practiced this completely. The Lord is calling His Body back to a whole salvation experience in body, soul and spirit, which is sanctification.

This is a three-part Godhead, redeeming His three-part man to overcome the flesh, the world and the devil. The reformation by Martin Luther defined salvation of the spirit by the scripture: *"the just shall live by faith."* This encompassed the redemptive action of God in the spirit of man and produced a consciousness of eternal life.

John Wesley reintroduced the sanctification of the soul and mind with his motto, "possessing the mind of Christ and all the mind of Christ." The motto's purpose was to focus the believer on his mind's purification, in order to bring his thoughts and habits into conformity with those of Christ.

The third part of the complete kingdom salvation is in the body. The results of wrong believing require redemption.

The ultimate purpose of healings and miracles is for man to walk in divine health. The healing and cleansing of the body from disease and sin is not simply another method of recovery from sickness, but is instead God's action to destroy all effects of sin and prepare the Christian for the indwelling of God Himself by the Holy Spirit.

> *You are cleansed and pruned already, because of the word, which I have given you.*
>
> JOHN 15:3

Jesus spoke these words to His disciples a few days before His crucifixion and their infilling on the day of Pentecost.

> *Now when the day of Pentecost had come, they were all with one accord in one place. Suddenly there came from the sky a sound like the rushing of a mighty wind, and it filled the entire house where they were sitting.*
> *Tongues like fire appeared and were distributed to them, and one sat on each of them. They were all filled with the Holy Spirit, and began to speak with other languages, as the Spirit gave them the ability to speak.*
>
> ACTS 2:1–4

The disciples had become qualified to carry God inside their beings because the water of the word (*Jesus*) had sanctified them wholly. In other words, each part of their beings had become holy. **Sin, sickness and disease destroy so many Christians because they have NOT exposed their spirits, souls, and body to the complete gospel of the kingdom or Jesus.**

The belief that Jesus died for our sins does not convert our souls and bodies. So the **reality** is, unless we wash our souls and bodies in Jesus, we will live a life in sickness and sinful habits, doubting the power of the Word. In the same way, that faith is the substance, which sustains belief; doubt is the **substance** that reinforces **unbelief**. The result is a person who is weak, depressed, beaten down and oppressed by the devil.

4. CENTERS OF MAN AS DEFINED BY JESUS

We are three-part beings — spirit, soul and body. Nevertheless, more revelation and understanding reveal two additional components of our triune being, the mind and heart.

Theologians in the past have taught that the mind and heart are part of the soul. Nevertheless, my research leads me to believe that they are vital connections between the spirit, soul and body and function independently. Believing as Jesus does depends on our understanding of each of these centers.

The purpose of this discussion is to rip away the veil of darkness hindering our understanding of the truth. If the devil can prevent any part of our centers from experiencing the light of Christ, our defeat is certain.

The diagrams illustrate each center's role as it pertains to sanctification. **(Refer to figures 1 & 2 on page 133 and 134)**

Look at what Jesus says to the theologians of His time.

> *And there came one of the scribes that had heard them reasoning together, and seeing that he had answered them well, asked him which was the first commandment of all.*
> *And Jesus answered him: The first commandment of all is, Hear, O Israel: the Lord thy God is one God.*
> *And thou shall **love** the Lord thy God with thy **whole heart** and with thy **whole soul** and with thy **whole mind** and with thy **whole strength**. This is the first commandment.*

*And the second is like to it: Thou shall love thy neigh-
bor as thyself. There is no other commandment greater
than these.*

MARK 12: 28–31

Each center Jesus identifies is the spiritual reflection of our
natural body. For example, **the spiritual heart is a reflection
of the physical heart, the soul is the spiritual reflection of
what a man believes, the mind is a spiritual representation
of the natural brain and so on.** In order for us to love God, our
spiritual structures must reproduce the substance or Christ
from each center.

Perfectly keeping the Laws of Moses was impossible until
Jesus did through the power of loving His Father. Jesus fulfilled the law by observing two commandments.

The Godhead is not jealous among itself over its purposes
and power. God is one, and as we learned, each of His characteristics is unique and vital to our sanctification.

This truth has helped me to identify the different persons
of the Godhead at work in my life. For example, I was minis-
tering one afternoon when I noticed a person in a wheelchair.
Ordinarily, I would not have focused on this person since I
was in the middle of my message, but I heard the voice of Jesus
saying, "Intercede for her right now." I obeyed, and the woman
began to move her legs in the chair. I did not have to stop the
service or lay hands on the person but only agree with the
intercessor of the universe.

**One of the most outstanding results of that meeting was
the intervention of both the Holy Spirit and Jesus simultaneously.** The Spirit led me during the message and Jesus our
intercessor interrupted me to pray. This is an example of God
the Son and God the Holy Ghost operating simultaneously but
differently.

71

The more sanctified my vessel becomes the easier it is to recognize the different persons of the Godhead at work in my being. The amazing thing to witness is how unique each one is but how united they are in purpose.

Jesus says we *must* — it is not an option — love God with all of our being, beginning with our heart.

A. DEFINITIONS AND FUNCTION OF THE HEART

The heart of man is the first place corrupted by the devil because of its importance. Love is the heavenly material degraded by the devil. The perversion of love is the single greatest weapon of the enemy. The heart is the doorway for belief, thoughts and impulses. It is not the physical organ but the spiritual apparatus, which contains the conscience.

The heart is the door that connects our spirits with our souls as we see in the illustration. **(Refer to figures 1 & 2 on pages 133 and 134).** If man recognizes God's voice as His Father via the heart, the Holy Spirit will release His power to transform the heart and awaken the spirit. **This process is salvation and begins with the heart, as described in Ezekiel.**

A new heart also will I give you, and a new spirit will I put within you; and I will take away the stony heart out of your flesh, and I will give you a heart of flesh.
I will put my Spirit within you, and cause you to walk in my statutes, and you shall keep my ordinances, and do them.

EZEKIEL 36:26–27

I will give them one heart, and put a new spirit within them; I will remove the heart of stone from their flesh and give them a heart of flesh.

EZEKIEL 11:19

The heart is tender while we are children but hardens as we are wounded, mistreated and betrayed. Over time, sin and unbelief create walls whose purpose is to protect us from pain; however, in reality they separate us from God and His voice and surround us with lies.

As I study the scripture, I am convinced the conscience resides in the heart of man. It is located in the heart not our spirit according to the scriptures. People are unable to hear God's voice without a tender conscience. Furthermore, without a pure heart we cannot access the faith, which resides in our spirits.

> *These people will speak lies disguised as truth. Their consciences have been scarred as if branded by a red-hot iron.*
> 1 TIMOTHY 4:2 (GOD'S WORD TRANSLATION)

> *Through the false ways of men whose words are untrue, whose hearts are burned as with a heated iron.*
> 1 TIMOTHY 4:2 (BASIC ENGLISH TRANSLATION)

> *May we draw near with a true heart, in full assurance of faith, having the hearts sprinkled from an evil conscience, and having the body bathed with pure water.*
> HEBREWS 10:22 (KING JAMES VERSION)

> *Blessed are the pure in heart: for they shall see God.*
> MATTHEW 5:8

> **Now the end of the commandment is love out of a pure heart, and of a good conscience, and of faith unfeigned:**
> 1 TIMOTHY 1:5

The ultimate weapon over the devil is the invisible substance of God or love. The instrument created in man to convert God's love from invisible to visible is the heart. A heart awakened by the love of God will transform a stony heart to one of flesh. Belief is the vehicle between the unseen and seen via the heart. The Holy Spirit uses the heart of flesh to believe all things.

> *I may have the gift to speak what God has revealed, and I may understand all mysteries and have all knowledge. I may even have enough faith to move mountains. But if I don't have love, I am nothing*
>
> 1 CORINTHIANS 13:2

> *Love bears all things, believeth all things, hopes all things, endures all things.*
>
> 1 CORINTHIANS 13:7

Dearly beloved, the most powerful weapon in the universe is love. Jesus created everything we can see with our natural eyes from the substance of **love. God is love, and He is the invisible substance that created everything visible.**

Therefore, our miracle depends on our believing with a heart whose substance is love, or Christ. **If we will love the way Jesus does, we will be able to believe the same way.** Love overwhelms anything and everything that resists it.

The understanding of the heart's operation is essential to enter true salvation.

> *That if with your mouth you confess Jesus as Lord and in your **heart believe** that God brought Him back to life, you shall be saved.*

*For with the heart men believe and obtain righteous-
ness, and with the mouth they make confession and
obtain salvation.*

ROMANS 10:9–10

The work of salvation is a process beginning with believing in the heart. I recited this scripture with my pastor when
first coming to Christ. However, although I felt the conviction of the Holy Spirit, my understanding was not clear. My
belief was, if I recited, "God raised Jesus from the dead" I
would be saved and going to heaven. After many years of
tribulations from horrible life choices, I finally studied the
difference between believing with the mind versus believing with the heart.

Believing with the mind may produce a moral person
but never a righteous one, according to Christ. I was not
even moral but considered myself a Christian because of a
wrong belief. Unfortunately, I have heard horror stories from
other precious brothers and sisters who experienced similar
results of hell because of wrong believing.

B. DEFINITIONS AND FUNCTION OF THE SOUL

The soul of man is that wonderful apparatus whose com-
plex operations are not fully understood. The center contains
our emotions, senses and will. **Man makes his decisions to
believe or not to believe information from there**.

The fall of man unseated the heart and spirit of man and
enthroned the soul. The centers for creativity and productiv-
ity by the leading of the Spirit are located within the emotions,
senses and will. The soul in the hands of the enemy is man's
ultimate downfall. The analogy of giving an atomic weapon to

a child is the essence of a soul without the leading of the Holy Ghost. The soul's ambition without Jesus is self-exaltation. **(Refer to figures 1 & 2 on pages 133 and 134)**

> *And thou shall love the Lord thy God with thy whole soul*
>
> MARK 12:30

The following is an example of hearts and souls united. The preaching of prosperity or unity is not necessary when this occurs.

> *The multitude of those who did believe the heart and the soul was one, and not one was saying that anything of the things he had was his own, but all things were to them in common.*
>
> ACTS 4:32

One of the noticeable evidences of the Spirit possessing the soul is the willingness to give. Self-survival becomes insignificant when compared to loving God. If we truly love Him, there is a release of every resource and structure holding our souls to the god of riches.

Each time the Lord comes to me with an appeal for time, money or material in my possession, joy floods my soul. **Selfishness is the evidence of a soul that contains more self than God.**

Unfortunately, the lack of spontaneity and generosity in giving like the early Church has provoked many Christian leaders to ask for money in ways that are grievous to the Holy Ghost.

For instance, many messages such as the "one hundred-fold return," manipulate persons to give by focusing on the reward from God. **There would be no need for methods unpleasing to our Lord if ministers could open the eyes of people to the riches of a soul connected to Christ.**

*And the multitude of them that believed were of **one
heart and of one soul**: neither said any of them that
ought of the things, which he possessed, was his own;
but they had all things common.*

*And with great power gave the apostles witness of the
resurrection of the Lord Jesus: and great grace was upon
them all.*

*Neither was there any among them that lacked: for as
many as were possessors of lands or houses sold them,
and brought the prices of the things that were sold,*

*And laid them down at the apostles' feet: and distribu-
tion was made unto men according as he had need.*

ACTS 4:32–35

**One heart and soul joined in Christ results in a divine
awakening to the invisible, which results in our release of
everything visible to obtain more of the invisible.** The dif-
ficulty for us has been how to produce this consciousness in
the multitudes. I believe the consciousness of Christ displays
the power of conversion to the masses through signs and
wonders.

Once we display Him, there is no need for sermons on
prosperity or anything else to incite people to follow Christ.
The invisible kingdom becomes visible through the manifestation of Jesus. It is only when this does not occur that the need
for soul activity is required.

The offices we find in Ephesians 4:11 are job descriptions
not titles. The desire for titles, popularity and position is not
important if the Lord chooses us to perform a duty. The job
descriptions written by Paul are real. Moreover, our titles will
be obvious as long as the Holy Ghost receives the honor for
the work. If we want job titles, it might be better to hear the
description Jesus gives to those who follow Him.

77

And whosoever will be chief among you, let him be your servant.

MATTHEW 20:27

Behold, my servant whom I have chosen; My beloved in whom my soul is well pleased: I will put my Spirit upon him, And he shall declare judgment to the Gentiles.

MATTHEW 12:18

Our soul will never demonstrate the power of God unless we conceive and understand the reality of the Christ as Jesus. In other words, **Jesus knew that only through His union with God could His soul become the sinless vessel that God would endorse with His power and authority.**

The Holy Spirit surging through our spirit, soul and bodies is the revelation of salvation. This is what Paul means when he says, *"Work out your own salvation with fear and trembling"* (Philippians 2:12).

C. DEFINING THE MIND

Scientists have determined that the Dutch people of the Netherlands are the tallest people on earth. **For the past fifty years, very interesting statistics reveal amazing phenomena concerning the power of the mind.** The Dutch people increased in height every year except the five years during the Second World War. During those years, the Germans occupied and oppressed the Dutch and research shows the race actually decreased in height. **This study reveals the extraordinary power of the mind and soul over the body.**

The mind is the center of intelligence, reason and memory and may resemble a computer with unlimited power and memory. **It displays the consciousness it believes through thinking and the body's behavior.**

Scientists believes the average human uses less than ten percent of the brain's capacity. **The mind is a physical instrument but has spiritual components that if activated by the Holy Spirit can be a miraculous device for inventions.**

Our souls must have the consciousness of Christ in order to control our minds' activity. **The *emotions* and *will* are but two of the important centers in the soul that control the mind.** The mind is a powerful computer, which if plugged into the Holy Spirit can harness that power to create kingdom solutions.

Many of the greatest inventions of modern man occurred after the great outpouring of the Holy Spirit in the early twentieth century. Any visitation by God will always bring prosperity for everyone.

> ***And thou shall love the Lord thy God with thy whole mind.***
>
> MARK 12:30

> *For if men are controlled by their earthly natures, they give their minds to earthly things. If they are controlled by their spiritual natures, they give their minds to spiritual things; because for the mind to be given up to earthly things means death; but for it to be given up to spiritual things means Life and peace. Abandonment to earthly things is a state of enmity to God. Such a mind does not submit to God's Law, and indeed cannot do so. And those whose hearts are absorbed in earthly things cannot please God.*
>
> ROMANS 8:5–7 WEYMOUTH

The general belief in the world today is that the mental supremacy of scientists will solve all of man's problems.

Therefore, the media and intellectuals go to great lengths to eliminate God as the omnipotent creator of mankind and Him alone as the **only solution** for our condition. In other words, man still wants to return to the mentality Adam obtained after the fall. In essence, man is saying, "I will make my own choice and be my own god."

The truth is, science has never created laws that govern our universe but only discover the principles of God, which keep everything in order. Moreover, anyone whose primary concern is self-survival is frightened at the thought of not being in control. Herein, lies the principal reason why man refuses to believe he does not have all the answers.

Man so easily believes the lie of the one who wants to destroy him and refuses to believe the One who has died for him in order to provide the truth.

Therefore, as we said earlier, **it does not matter if what the mind believes is true or not; it merely reacts to the information it receives from the other centers.** Therefore, if the Holy Spirit has joined our souls to Christ, the mind will be a creative force for building God's kingdom. On the other hand, the soul will display images dominated by fear and doubt if untransformed.

For example, if someone unknown moves into a neighborhood and their appearance or demeanor differs from the average homeowner, suspicion and fear will create images derived from the latest crime statistics. The person may or may not present a threat, but to the unconverted mind, this person could be a serial killer.

Believing lies and false statements is easier because of our conditioning from television and other sources dominated by this world's system. The truth however will make us dependent on Jesus while lies only give us a temporary false sense of superiority.

Think about it for a minute. Most information we hear or see is not positive, but rather negative. **Therefore, our conscious minds, in order to be secure and protect the ego or pride, will assume the worse in nearly all situations.** To the unconverted soul being right even at the expense of someone else's reputation is always more self-gratifying than believing that *"all things to work for the good"* (Romans 8:28).

The mind is the devil's chalkboard. He uses pictures, sounds and impressions in ways to frighten and control the heart and soul. One reason we are afraid is that fear **believes** lies. The lie is the silver cord that keeps us bound to our **realities of sin, sickness and death.**

For instance, if the Holy Spirit does not possess our heart, soul and mind, we will become frightened if we continually hear about a strain of flu that threatens to infect the whole world. **The fear will ultimately become an image in our minds, manifesting the symptoms in our bodies.**

The reason that we sin is the same reason that we become sick. We surrender to the suggestion of the devil. The thought takes root in the heart, usually through fear, and progresses through all man's centers until manifesting in the body.

The Bible is the only tool capable of penetrating each center with the truth and grace of Christ.

> *For the word of God is living and full of power, and is sharper than any two-edged sword, cutting through and making a division even of the soul and the spirit, the bones and the muscles, and quick to see the thoughts and purposes of the heart.*
>
> HEBREWS 4:12

The word is Jesus. His word is the power to convert the mind to Christ in order for us to know God. Once we truly know God, the mind looses its desire for self-preservation and transcends to its original purpose, which is to serve the Spirit. Beloved, there is a consciousness in Christ that rises above this life with its petty ambitions into real kingdom authority. That is the beginning of the mind of Christ.

> *For who has knowledge of the mind of the Lord, so as to be his teacher? But we have the mind of Christ.*
> 1 CORINTHIANS 2:16

> *And be renewed in the **spirit of** your mind;*
> EPHESIANS 4:23

In my opinion, the result of a heart, soul and mind filled with the love and knowledge of **Christ is a consciousness or intelligence that will remain after death**. The consciousness of Christ is the eternal overcomer of death. I am **not** speaking about the physical body. **I am talking about the consciousness of Christ, which possess a mind beyond the grave**.

Paul is speaking about a mind in Ephesians 4:23 that is capable of communicating with God outside of time. Therefore, if Jesus is capable of understanding our feelings because He can **remember** what it is like to be tempted and not sin (Hebrews 4:15), then I believe He made a way for you and me to experience the same victory.

Why was it possible for Jesus to go into hell and recover what Adam lost? **I believe it was because His consciousness encompassed the grave**. The purpose in speaking about this subject is to challenge the way we perceive our life as Christians. The popular notion that only after Jesus returns will we reign victoriously is a lie from the devil. **The authority of the Christ consciousness is now and goes beyond this life and the grave**. Our spirit connected with His Spirit will reveal unspeakable treasures.

I think this is what Paul is alluding to in the following scriptures.

...who hath been made, not after the law of a carnal commandment, but after the power of an endless life.
HEBREWS 7:16

*Therefore then, since **we are** surrounded by so great a cloud of witnesses...*
HEBREWS 12:1 (AMPLIFIED)

I believe those whose souls and spirits are so united in Christ that they will have been in heaven many times before their physical death. Therefore, their experiences and belief accompany them in order to rule and reign for the ages to come.

My reason for mentioning this is to challenge all our belief systems and shift our paradigms. Exploring the Bible as never before is one of the results of new revelations and leaving our comfort zones. If you approach the scriptures with a pure heart to see God and **are not** motivated by any other reason than knowing the Father the way Jesus did, the Holy Spirit will protect you from going astray. Problems will arise for those whose goals are not pure.

Each time the Lord has allowed me to visit Him in heaven; my mind changes to understand His Word in a deeper way. For example, the Lord took me to heaven and I heard Him repeat what He said in Matthew 8:22: *Follow me; and let the dead bury their dead.*

Immediately, I observed people, who appeared dead, walking with a dark shroud over their eyes. They were attempting to remove the veil, very oblivious to others standing around them who were shining like light. Upon closer investigation, I could see that some of the people who were shining resembled what I pictured Jesus looking like while he was on the mountain during His transfiguration. The Spirit reminded me that Jesus was able to see and talk with Elijah and Moses during that encounter.

I began to meditate on that experience, and I truly believe Jesus was allowing me to see an example of intelligence after death. Moses had asked God to see His glory. That desire had so consumed Moses that God resurrected him from the bosom of Abraham to fulfill his heart's desire in the person of Jesus. **The thoughts and desires originating from the Spirit if allowed to penetrate our minds via the heart and soul will leave an everlasting imprint in our minds and bodies**.

> *And it came to pass, as they were burying a man and when the man was let down, and touched the bones of Elisha, he revived, and stood up on his feet.*
>
> 2 KINGS 13:21

D. THE BODY

The mind filled with Christ has, as a bonus, a body completely free from disease. The physical body of man does not sin because **the will to sin is in the soul**. Of course, this instrument is responsible for acting out of most sins. Nevertheless, the body itself cannot make the decision to sin.

> *Flee from fornication. Any other sin that a human being commits lies outside the body; but he who commits fornication sins against his own body.*
>
> 1 CORINTHIANS 6:18

God created the body to obey the mind, soul and heart. Once the Holy Spirit is in control, every disease and sickness will disappear. Jesus showed us the greatest example of a body so filled with God's glory that even His clothes shone on the mount of Transfiguration.

And he said to them, "Truly I tell you, there are some
standing here who will not taste death until they see
that the kingdom of God has come with power."
Six days later, Jesus took with him Peter and James and
John, and led them up a high mountain apart, by them-
selves. And he was transfigured before them,
and his clothes became dazzling white, such as no one
on earth could bleach them.

MARK 9:1–3

Jesus tells His disciples that few will see the power of the
kingdom before they physically die. He then takes three disciples to the mountaintop to show them that He is the kingdom
and the power and the glory. Moses and Elijah appear representing the law and the prophets to witness the glory of God. **Jesus**
shines brighter than the noonday sun, demonstrating the
glorification and coming resurrection of the Christ. In other
words, Jesus had not only sanctified but also glorified every center of His being to the point that even His clothes radiated.

This picture of Jesus overflowing with the Holy Ghost in
every center of His being should be the desire of every heart.
The Holy Ghost must have complete and unhindered access to
the heart, soul, mind and body. This manifestation is not only
available to those who desire Him but also is a requirement
for those who want to believe as He does. There is no shadow
in this glory; shadows are the places of doubt and unbelief.
Beyond all words and miracles, Jesus showed Peter, James and
John the way to become victorious over everything on earth.
In essence, God pours Himself into the sanctified container,
Jesus. Sanctifying the container is a job for the Holy Spirit,
but it requires our death in every area of our being.

His Father validates the power of this picture when He
says, *"Hear him."* In other words, listen only to **Him** if you want
transformation and transfiguration in every cell of your being.

The power residing in the words of Christ will transform every part of our beings.

Jesus gives us the key to how to reach this level when He speaks about the two greatest commandments.

> *And the second is like the first, namely this; you shall love your neighbor as yourself. There is none other commandments greater than these.*
>
> *And the scribe said unto him, Well, Master, thou hast said the truth: for there is one God; and there is none other but he: And to love him with all the heart, and with all the understanding, and with all the soul, and with all the strength, and to love his neighbor as himself, is more than all whole burnt offerings and sacrifices.*
>
> *And when Jesus saw that he gave a wise answer, he said to him, **you are not far from the kingdom of God**. And every man after that was in fear of questioning him any more.*
>
> MARK 12: 31–34

The reason he was not far from the kingdom is that he had not entered into the words of Jesus. Jesus is the kingdom of God. Unless we enter into Him, we will still be on the outside of His kingdom. **Because of the first Adam, we are all born into the kingdom of this world, controlled by the devil. That is why we must renounce this kingdom in order to enter His kingdom.**

We spoke before about how the world forms its belief systems from the framework of lawlessness. Moses instituted the laws of God to establish a foundation for righteousness. The High priest made sacrifices for the sins of the people because the law was impossible to keep.

E. LOVE, THE FORCE THAT UNITES

Jesus came on the scene and perfectly fulfilled the law and established only two commandments. Then He explained that the only way to keep them is through the supremacy of love.

Love is the power the Holy Ghost uses to start the transformation. First, love changes our stony hearts into flesh, and then leads us through sanctification of the soul and mind, with the eventual healing of our bodies. This magnificent process establishes our relationship with the Father. But it does not stop with us; it never does. We must love our neighbor with the same enthusiasm that the Holy Ghost has loved us. Our relationship with the Father carries a demand: that we be responsible for others.

> *But he, desirous of justifying himself, said to Jesus, and who is my **neighbor**?*
>
> *And Jesus replying said, a certain man descended from Jerusalem to Jericho and fell into the hands of robbers, who also, having stripped him and inflicted wounds, went away leaving him in a half-dead state. And a certain **priest** happened to go down that way, and seeing him, passed on the opposite side; and in like manner also a **Levite**, being at the spot, came and looked [at him] and passed on the opposite side. But a certain **Samaritan** journeying came to him, and seeing him, was moved with compassion, and came up to him and bound up his wounds, pouring in oil and wine; and having put him on his own beast, took him to the inn and took care of him. And on the morrow as he left, taking out two pennies he gave them to the innkeeper, and said to him, Take care of him, and whatsoever thou shall expend more, I will render to thee on my coming back.*

Which now of these three seems to thee to have been
neighbor of him who fell into the hands of the robbers?
And he said, He that showed him mercy. And Jesus said
to him, Go, and do thou likewise.

LUKE 10:29–37

The religious men illustrated in this parable never impressed Jesus. The Samaritans were people with whom the Jews did not even associate. Yet, those who lived by the law were not as righteous as the Samaritan was. **Jesus was demonstrating the kingdom principles of love and righteousness that fulfill the law.**

Redemption must occur in every part of man's spirit, soul and body in order to believe like Jesus. Our reality must be that of the kingdom of God. The goal of the Holy Spirit is to completely transform us into the likeness of Christ, who is the kingdom of God. If you are not experiencing the supernatural life of the kingdom in each center of your being, then I want to pray with you.

Holy Spirit, the same way you opened my eyes to the truth of your glorious purification process in every area of my being, I am asking you to do the same for the person praying this prayer. Even now, quicken their spirits Lord to the truth of who you are. Lord, you are so precious, and I humbly ask you to touch this dear person right where they are, this instant. Thank you Jesus, Amen.

Chapter Five

Entering Christ

1. PURSUING CHRIST

Most of my adult life has been in the pursuit of Christ. I have heard different doctrines and beliefs from many Christians. One thing that has struck me is the number of doctrines that have focused on the future events of the Church. My purpose is not to dispute the doctrines but to reposition our focus.

The Church appears to have been lulled to sleep by the promise of power in the future. Nevertheless, the release of the power the Church has been waiting on has already taken place.

> *Verily, verily, I say unto you, The hour is coming, and* ***now is****, when the dead shall hear the voice of the Son of God: and they that hear shall live.*
>
> JOHN 5:25

> ***Now is*** *the judgment of this world: now shall the prince of this world be cast out.*
>
> JOHN 12:31

> *Indeed, the time is coming, and **it is now here**, when the true worshipers will worship the Father in spirit and truth. The Father is looking for people like that to worship him.*
>
> JOHN 4:23

In these three scriptures alone we find everlasting life, power over the devil and God looking for worshippers **now**. It appears to me, the overcoming power we have been expecting in the future is available now. Jesus Christ will return as spoken by the angels on his ascent back to heaven. But He is coming to sit on His throne.

The reality is all the necessary tools needed to subdue the enemy and establish the kingdom are in the Bible and the Holy Ghost. Unfortunately, many churches since Biblical times have decided to believe doctrines that, instead of destroying mediocrity, nurture it, as demonstrated in the following scripture.

> *They will appear to have a godly life, but they will not let its power change them. Stay away from such people.*
>
> 2 TIMOTHY 3:5

The season in which we live is demanding a new generation to arise and take the lead. **The Joshua's and Caleb's must leave those who will die in the wilderness and sound the alarm to those who know their Lord.** We are at war, but just as in Jesus' day, the worst enemies are the ones inside the churches.

Certainly many churches and leaders are speaking out. Nevertheless, the mainstream denominations and many popular voices on Christian television are rocking the Church to sleep with psychological and nursery rhyme messages. Sermons designed to comfort, entertain and sustain the status quo.

Most of the world believes that Christianity is just another philosophy or religion to help society be moral. Jesus did not only come to save souls but to save men in their totality. He came to rescue our bodies from sickness, souls from sin and our spirits from eternal damnation.

Therefore, He gave eternal life with Him to the spirit, peace by redemption to the soul and healing to the body. This is the kingdom message, righteousness for the spirit, peace for the soul and joy for the body.

Therefore, the purpose of God through Christ is not morality but immortality, man transfigured, transformed and transmuted in the substance and likeness of Jesus. A definition of transmuted is to change or alter in form, appearance or nature to a higher form. This is the consciousness that Jesus possessed, in order to believe like His Father.

We must settle it forever that our lives will become in all aspects like Jesus Christ regardless of the price. That means we are not to hope for a future transformation but instead change now our spirit, soul and body. Otherwise, our belief is just another philosophy.

2. SOTERIA

Soteria is the Greek word that describes the transformation of Jesus into the Christ, which the cross of Calvary accomplished. This is both our example and inheritance from the Lord. The Bible says if we suffer with Him, we also will reign (2 Timothy 2:12).

Therefore, in order for our lives to become the conduit for the supernatural supply of heaven to manifest on earth, we all need to know Christ in a deeper dimension.

Do you know what makes Christianity the most powerful belief system throughout the universe? These days, the world is full of psychological and philosophical religions whose purpose is to sound religious and impress the mental appetites of men. **We must know beyond any doubt the difference between true Christianity and philosophies**.

Many of the world's religious teachings were already around when Jesus was born. The *Bhagavad-Gita*, the sacred book of Hinduism, was around eight hundred years before Isaiah. Buddha and Confucius, to name a couple, lived five hundred years before Jesus. The written texts of their beliefs sometimes even resembled those taught by Jesus, but they died without any future revelations. The same is true of Muhammad, the prophet of the Muslims; Joseph Smith, the leader of the Mormons; and any other philosophers who may become popular. The grave was and will be the end of their work and revelations.

Not Jesus, **Christianity begins at the grave, where all the other philosophies end**. Jesus not only rose from the dead, **but also determined in His soul to capture death**. Therefore, He entered death itself and took the power that binds man's soul, **the fear of death itself**. Moreover, He conquered the power over sin whose consequence is death in hell apart from God. Do you see it? The early Church spoke much more about this part of His ministry than the Church today. We see His majesty and power when He reveals Himself to John in the book of Revelation.

I died; but I am now alive until the Ages of the Ages,
and I have the keys of the gates of Death and of Hades!
REVELATION 1:18

Scientists have compared the power that God needed to raise Jesus from the dead to that of a nuclear explosion multiplied by one hundred. But death was no match for the consciousness of the Son of God. **Jesus was not only interested in resurrection but also in repossessing all the power structures, which held man captive since the day of his fall, including our believing.**

He returned from the dead with the consciousness of God along with His power and ability to command all things. None of the philosophers ever knew about that power or possessed it themselves. **Jesus made faith a fact, divine knowledge, and His vision was now His consciousness.**

All of the triumph and victory He obtained by overcoming Hell and death was blown into the faces of His disciples when He said, *"receive the Holy Ghost"* (John 20:22). **Death's power was broken in their consciousness as a result, because the same men, who days before ran frightened for their lives, shook the known world with His gospel and power.**

It does not end there; if it did, it would just be a better philosophy. Statements of belief do not make one a Christian anymore than sleeping in a garage makes one an automobile. **The secret of Christianity and salvation is our death and Christ's resurrection in us. He said receive Me, not as I was but as I am now, Glorified, Triumphant, Prophetic, Overcoming and King. This is what makes a Believer**—not reciting a particular passage or statement as a sinner's prayer.

Salvation occurs when there is a conscious knowing of Christ entering into the spirit of man. Jesus gives Himself to the heart, soul and mind of everyone who releases possession of his or her life. The believer is conscious of this exchange.

Have you ever seen Buddha, Confucius or any other philosopher enter anyone? **The reality of a person is in the consciousness or substance of their soul. In other words, our beliefs will always reflect the source that dominates our thoughts. Every philosophy or religion is powerless and empty when compared to the glorified majestic Christ.**

Therefore, all of Christianity lies inside the framework of the supernatural. Philosophies are all natural. But Jesus not only saves us from our sins but also changes our very nature so that we can become like Him. Think about it: Jesus can take you and me and make a real Son of God, complete with all His overcoming characteristics. The way that Jesus watched His

Father, in order to reflect His image, is the pattern that we are to follow as well.

I believe a real conversion experience occurs when the spirit awakens in man to the consciousness of the Fatherhood of God through Jesus Christ. The conscious union with God requires the removal of everything preventing the knowledge and love of God.

Sin is what veils the soul and conceals God from our consciousness. Jesus destroyed any hold that sin could legally have on the consciousness of man. Therefore, man is at liberty to choose his master. The choice we make determines our life now and after death. If we can see God as our Father even in a brief encounter, love will flood our spirits and bring us into union with God. **That meeting with heaven brings with it a consciousness that is beyond philosophies and religion. Love pours forth and floods our souls with the reality of our absolute helplessness without Jesus.**

This is the beginning of salvation. The redemption of man and salvation commences when the soul and mind of man enter into the Spirit of God. The result of that experience is the awakening into the kingdom of God.

> *You are receiving the outcome of your faith, the salvation of your souls.*
>
> 1 PETER 1:9

The salvation of our souls occurs when the redemption from self is completed. The ego and pride of man is the mask of the devil. The cross of Christ is the ultimate humiliation of mankind. No other single event in history illustrates man's ego more fully than that of killing an innocent person. **The very Son of God says that those who wish to be His disciples will have to take up their cross. In other words, put your ego on display for all of mankind to humiliate and deface in order to enter His kingdom.**

ENTERING THE KINGDOM

The supernatural progression into the knowledge of Christ is the entrance to the kingdom. Salvation is a continual process in our spirit, soul and body until the consciousness arises within us to see the kingdom of God. The visual validation of the kingdom is the evidence of being "born again." The process is different in each person, but the results are the same. A new creature emerges with the characteristics of Christ.

To be "born again" is much deeper and profound than what most evangelicals describe to a new convert. **The truth is, denominations and religions have separated themselves by terminology and doctrine instead of uniting by the demonstration and power of Christ.**

The early Church received the living Christ and became a new creature. **Most churches today train people in their minds to receive concepts and formulas, which may produce morality but certainly not immortality or a new birth.**

One needs only to read the dialogue that Jesus has with Nicodemus to see clearly His definition of being born again.

> *He came to Jesus by night and said to him, Rabbi, we are certain that you have come from God as a teacher, because no man would be able to do these signs which you do if God was not with him.*
> *Jesus said to him, Truly, I say to you, **without a new birth no man is able to see the kingdom of God.***
> *Nicodemus said to him, How is it possible for a man to be given birth when he is old? Is he able to go into his mother's body a second time and come to birth again?*
> *Jesus said in answer, **Truly, I say to you, If a man's birth is not from water and from the Spirit, it is not possible for him to go into the kingdom of God.***

95

> *That which has birth from the flesh is flesh, and*
> *that which has birth from the Spirit is spirit.*
> *Do not be surprised that I say to you, It is necessary for*
> *you to have a second birth.*
> *The wind goes where its pleasure takes it, and*
> *the sound of it comes to your ears, but you are*
> *unable to say where it comes from and where it*
> *goes: so it is with everyone whose birth is from*
> *the Spirit.*
> *And Nicodemus said to him, How is it possible for these*
> *things to be?*
> *And Jesus, answering, said, Are you the teacher of Israel*
> *and have no knowledge of these things?*
> *Truly, I say to you, We say that of which we have knowl-*
> *edge; we give witness of what we have seen; and you do*
> *not take our witness to be true.*
> *If you have no belief when my words are about*
> *the things of earth, how will you have belief if*
> *my words are about the things of heaven?*
>
> JOHN 3:2–12

If we read this passage correctly, Jesus is explaining how we are to be born again, and the result of that experience. First, water and spirit are the elements used in the new birth. Second, we are able to see the kingdom.

The breaking of water inside the mother's womb commonly precedes childbirth. Nicodemus understood that part of birthing but was perplexed about the spirit.

The passage that reads *"that which has birth from the flesh is flesh, and that which has birth from the Spirit is spirit"* specifically describes the new birth into the kingdom of God. The birth into the spirit or kingdom is like the wind. We know it is real because we hear it and see the results but are unable to describe the physical characteristics.

Then Nicodemus asks what every creature outside the kingdom asks: *How?* Jesus answers with the same question He is asking us today: *"If you do not believe when I speak about simple things, how will you believe when I tell you about heavenly things?"*

The born again experience is a profound conscious act that commences when the Holy Spirit unites with the spirit of man. The seed of Christ will give birth if immersed in the characteristics of the Godhead. Then the same way the mother births the earthly child, the Holy Spirit, which has been described as maternal, births us into the kingdom.

> *No one born (begotten) of God [deliberately, knowingly, and habitually] practices sin, for God's nature abides in him [His principle of life, the divine sperm, remains permanently within him]; and he cannot practice sinning because he is born (begotten) of God.*
>
> *By this it is made clear who take their nature from God and are His children and who take their nature from the devil and are his children: no one who does not practice righteousness [who does not conform to God's will in purpose, thought, and action] is of God; neither is anyone who does not love his brother (his fellow believer in Christ).*
>
> 1 JOHN 3:9–10 (AMPLIFIED)

We are describing the vital importance of changing our belief systems in order to enter the kingdom of God. My birth into it was the result of my death to this world. The first evidence we have is a **visual experience** into the realms of God. *"No one can see the kingdom if He is not born again."* In fact, I also have had sensations of sound, taste and smells in the kingdom. The more conscious I become in Him the more profound are the experiences of the kingdom.

I believe Peter also had an experience of the kingdom when the Father revealed Jesus to him. Revelation is a mechanism used by the Spirit to plant the seed of Christ into our hearts.

> *Now when Jesus came into the district of Caesarea Philippi, he asked his disciples, who do people say that the Son of Man is?*
> *And they said, Some say John the Baptist, but others Elijah, and still others Jeremiah or one of the prophets.*
> *He said to them, But who do you say that I am?*
> *Simon Peter answered;* **You are the Christ, the Son of the living God.**
> *And Jesus answered him, Blessed are you, Simon son of Jonah! For flesh and blood has not revealed this to you, but my Father in heaven.*
> **And I tell you, you are Peter, and on this rock I will build my church, and the gates of Hades will not prevail against it.**
>
> MATTHEW 16:13–18

Jesus asks each of us along the path of our development the same question He asked His disciples. *"Whom do you say I am?"* The answer to this question will be different for each person, but it is vital if we are to enter the kingdom of God.

BOTH SPIRIT AND SOUL MUST ENTER THE KINGDOM OF GOD

We began our discussion defining believe and how it relates to our current conditions. All of us reflect daily the realities of our beliefs. But Jesus is still asking His disciples to tell Him who He is. (We discussed the definition of a disciple at length.)

Of course Jesus was much more interested in who His disciples thought He was than he was in the popular opinion of others. The scripture illustrates the duality of Peter's spirit and is a vivid picture of our own dilemma. Peter demonstrates how a person can enter the kingdom through revelation in his spirit one minute and then, immediately leave the kingdom, by processing the revelation in his soul and mind.

> *Then He warned the disciples that they should tell no one that He was the Christ.*
> *From that time Jesus Christ began to show His disciples that He must go to Jerusalem, and suffer many things from the elders and chief priests and scribe and be killed, and be raised up on the third day.*
> *And Peter took Him aside and began to rebuke Him, saying, God forbid it, Lord! This shall never happen to you.*
> *But He turned and said to Peter, Get behind Me, Satan! You are a stumbling block to me; for you are not setting your mind on God's interests, but man's.*
> MATTHEW 16: 20–23

Here is another instance which reveals Peter's reaction from his soul rather than his spirit.

> *Six days later, Jesus took with Him Peter, James, and John, and brought them alone, apart from the rest, up a high mountain; and in their presence His appearance underwent a change. His garments also became dazzling with brilliant whiteness—such whiteness as no bleaching on earth could give.*
> *Moreover there appeared to them Elijah accompanied by Moses; and the two were conversing with Jesus, when Peter said to Jesus, Rabbi, we are thankful to you that we are here. Let us put up three tents—one for you, one*

*for Moses, and one for Elijah. For **he knew not what to say**: they were filled with such awe.*
*there came a cloud spreading over them, and a voice issued from the cloud, This is my Son, dearly loved: **listen to Him**.*

MATTHEW 17:1–5

The fact that Peter wanted to build three tabernacles illustrates many things, but the most important is that his spirit, not his soul, identified Jesus as the Christ. **This is an example of how we can say one thing by revelation and believe something entirely different in our souls. The soul always wants to talk and surround itself with noise because it is uncomfortable with silence. Therefore, God the Father has to say, in essence, be still and be quiet and *listen* only to my Son.**

The revelation of Christ in our spirit and soul is the birth into the kingdom of God. Peter did not understand that initially, but the reality of Peter's conversion into the kingdom was visible after Pentecost (Acts 2:6–7). *They were greatly surprised because every man was hearing the words of the disciples in his special language. And they were full of wonder and said, are not all these men Galileans?*

> *Everyone who believes that Jesus is the Christ has been born of God.*
>
> 1 JOHN 5:1

Unfortunately, not everyone who thinks he believes knows what it means. The more we understand the word **believe** the more obvious it becomes that we do not fully comprehend the meaning and absoluteness of that word. To **believe** describes an immoveable, unshakeable trust in the knowledge of the person of Christ.

The revelation of Christ is the material of the rock. The rock is the immoveable foundation of the Church. The gates of hell cannot prevail against the substances or materials from heaven. The prophetic voice is the foundation, not flesh and blood. That foundation will stop hell and advance the kingdom.

Jesus spoke the parable of the men who built their homes on rock and sand. Jesus compared the one who obeyed Him to building on a rock, while the disobedient one built on the sand.

The revelation of Christ *(the rock)* **compels us to obedience, which creates inside us His substance**. The substance of Christ within us will reveal our character and whom it is we believe and trust.

Jesus tells Peter that, in essence, that revelation and prophecy are the foundation for entering the kingdom. **The Spirit will birth us into His kingdom.** Regrettably, the prophetic is not part of most churches. Consequently, we have religious "flesh and blood" systems instead of a prophetic church destroying hell and death by the spirit of prophecy.

> *For the testimony of Jesus is the spirit of prophecy.*
> REVELATION 19:10

The persons who are trapped in systems and perishing due to wrong believing break my heart. **The Lord has stirred me to tell those of you who are in such a place, to "Get out of there now" and find out for yourselves who Jesus is through the Holy Spirit.**

You will never be able to help your friends in those churches unless you first find the answer yourself. The power of that revelation alone will give you the authority of heaven and earth.

The reality of Christ is not something we will find from anyone else. Places and people will often be a tool used by the Holy Ghost to help, but ultimately it will be between you and Jesus.

The revelation of Christ is the first step into the kingdom and from that point forward you must depend on and believe only the Holy Spirit. This is why wrong belief systems will hinder you from hearing and obeying the Holy Spirit. Our erroneous beliefs prevent most of us from a deeper revelation of Christ. The Holy Ghost is the author of revelation and ALL TRUTH. He will lead us into the reality of Christ.

> *But when He, the Spirit of Truth (the Truth-giving Spirit) comes, He will guide you into all the Truth (the whole, full Truth). For He will not speak His own message on His own authority; but He will tell whatever He hears from the Father; He will give the message that has been given to Him, and He will announce and declare to you the things that are to come that will happen in the future.*
>
> JOHN 16:13

Jesus had to rebuke His disciples because of their unbelief on many occasions. This restricted Him from showing them the depth of His overcoming consciousness when He described future events.

> *Jesus saw that they had a desire to put the question to him, so he said to them, Is this what you are questioning one with another, why I said, After a little time, you will see me no longer; and then again, after a little time, you will see me?*
> *Truly I say to you, you will be weeping and sorrowing, but the **world will be glad:** you will be sad, **but your sorrow will be turned into joy.***
> ***When a woman is about to give birth she has sorrow,** because her hour is come; but when she has given birth to the child, the pain is put out of her mind*

*by the joy that a man has come into the world. So you have sorrow now: but I will see you again, and your hearts will be glad, and **no one will take away your joy. Up to now you have made no request in my name: do so, and it will be answered, so that your hearts may be full of joy.***

JOHN 16:19–22, 24

Jesus was explaining the mystery by which all men would enter the kingdom of God. The analogy of a woman giving birth was not just a coincidence but also a visual picture of the process necessary for us to see Him. **The sorrow we all experience is the natural reaction of repentance when we come to Jesus by the Holy Spirit.**

All men, as descendants of the first Adam, are responsible for His crucifixion. However, that sorrow turns to joy when our hearts see Jesus through true believing. Then we can ask in His name, because we know Him and it will be answered.

If you are asking in His name without receiving what you ask, it could very well be that you believe only in your mind. Most people believe God raised Jesus from the dead.

Now we know that you know everything. You don't need to wait for questions to be asked. Because of this, we believe that you have come from God. Jesus replied to them, now you believe.

JOHN 16:30–31

Our unbelief always limits Jesus. The mind is a continual battleground that unless submitted to the control of the Holy Spirit will be our destruction.

Jesus tells Peter, *"I am giving you the keys to the kingdom of heaven."* Why would Jesus offer the keys to someone whom He had to rebuke and a few weeks later would deny Him? **God** is after Sons and is willing to trust us with the keys to His kingdom in order to examine our hearts.

The good news is that if we belong to Him, we cannot fail the examination. The bad news is that we must keep taking the test until we pass. I can recall early in my Christian life taking the same test many times. The following is an example of one of my ordeals.

I supported many famous ministries for various reasons but primarily because of my hunger for a spectacular demonstration of God's power. For years, I would attend large conferences with several thousand people. My goal was for the minister to see me. Sitting in the front row increased the chances of fulfilling my ambition. Unfortunately, most of those who attended these events also had the same desire. **The physical location became more important than the spiritual position of my heart.**

The truth was that I was more interested in the attention of men and the appearance of being "spiritual." Therefore, I did whatever was necessary to obtain those seats. Most of the time this meant lie, cheat and anything short of fist fighting. How holy this all must have looked to the Lord!

One day, the Holy Spirit asked me. "Do you love me?" "Of course, I do" was my response. "Then sit in the very back of the auditorium tonight and do not move even if called," He said. The Lord then directed my attention to a little old lady in the back row who was on her knees praying. She appeared to be unaware of the events on the stage. She was crying out to God in such a way that people were asking her to be quiet.

The Lord said, "**Those who do not know me believe there is a shortcut. However, those who are passionate for me are not satisfied with someone else's knowledge of me. That lady is passionate for Me.** "

My immaturity devastated me. I began to question my salvation. My repentance persisted for most of the night. It was not until I had determined that nothing was going to hinder me from knowing Christ that peace came and that test ended.

The revelation we receive at every level will always test us, as well as reveal our character. Many times those whose souls and minds are not sanctified will be destroyed by the gifts of God.

Jesus told Peter that satan desired to sift him as wheat. Paul received a thorn because of the revelation from the Holy Ghost. Revelation will get the attention of the enemy, and God will use the devil so that He can sanctify us. Peter and Paul are two examples of that principle.

The revelation of Christ will start a work inside your being that will crystallize much of what you have read to now. I pray that the Holy Ghost will speak to you right now about the level of Christ that has permeated your spirit, soul and body.

A DRINK FROM THE LIVING WELL

The Holy Spirit wants to open our eyes so that we may understand the difference between salvation and entering the kingdom. It is through a divine encounter with a Samaritan woman that Jesus unfolded the truth between the two.

Jesus was leaving Judea because the religious leaders wanted to create jealousy among the believers. It is interesting to note that rather than defend Himself Jesus left. **So often people are more interested in staying in a religious setting to defend their self-image instead of leaving for the unknown to be formed by the Spirit.**

> *Therefore when the Lord knew that the Pharisees had heard that Jesus was making and baptizing more disciples than John (although Jesus himself didn't baptize, but his disciples), he left Judea, and departed into Galilee.*
>
> JOHN 4:1–4

Jesus is physically tired and thirsty and decides to sit by a well in Samaria, and asks a woman of Samaria to give him a drink. However, the Lord was asking for something much more than water. Let the Holy Spirit take you to a different depth of understanding of this passage.

> *Jesus therefore, being tired from his journey, sat down by the well. It was about the sixth hour. **A woman of Samaria came to draw water. Jesus said to her, give me a drink**. For his disciples had gone away into the city to buy food. The Samaritan woman therefore said to him, how is it that you, being a Jew, ask for a drink from me, a Samaritan woman? (For Jews have no dealings with Samaritans.) Jesus answered her, if you knew the gift of God, and whom it is who says to you, Give me a drink, you would have asked him, and he would have given you living water.*
>
> JOHN 4:5–10

Jesus is coming to your well right now to ask you for your resources of strength. Our wells may be popularity, status, money; knowledge of the Bible and any other thing that we believe is our security. Jesus is asking for it today. He tells us why in verse 10.

> *Jesus answered her, **If you knew the gift of God, and whom it is who says to you, Give me a drink, you would have asked him, and he would have given you living water.***
>
> JOHN 4:10

But you say, "I know Jesus, He is my savior and Lord." Is He? What do you believe and why do you believe what you believe? Is what you believe **sufficient** to supply your every need and that of a dying world?

Sadly, many of the Christians today are so content with their lifestyles or "wells" that they do not recognize Jesus. Therefore, He is asking us to give to Him our security and strengths, or our belief systems. Perhaps this is why so many pastors preach about giving.

> *The woman said to him, Sir, you have nothing to draw with, and the well is deep. From where then have you that living water? Are you greater than our father, Jacob, who gave us the well, and drank of it himself, as did his children, and his cattle?* Jesus answered her, Everyone who drinks of this water will thirst again, but *whoever drinks of the water that I will give him will never thirst again; but the water that I will give him will become in him a well of water springing up to eternal life.* The woman said to him, Sir, give me this water, so that I don't get thirsty, neither come all the way here to draw.
>
> JOHN 4:11–15

The woman's response is similar to many today whose belief is in the reality of this world as their resource, rather than Jesus. Many Christians believe the "wells of Jacob" are sufficient to supply all their needs. After all, Jacob is the grandson of Abraham, one of the wealthiest men in the scriptures.

Many church messages speak about the prosperity of Abraham as proof of faith. This is a subtle diversion from the living water of Christ to the natural provision of this world. **Therefore, unless we meet the living Christ we will not desire to drink from an unfamiliar well.**

Religions and society will always question methods, ideologies, histories and anything else, that challenges the status quo. In other words, how can you possess the truth if you do not dress, talk, sing or look anything like what I believe? **The world is drinking from religions and dying of thirst.**

The topic of living water is reminiscent of the conversation that Jesus had with Nicodemus. Jesus told Nicodemus in order to be born again he must be born of water and spirit.

Jesus is the living water. He tells us that eternal life begins after we drink from Him. The more of Him we drink, the faster we are conformed into His image.

Jesus told the Samaritan woman that she needed to drink living water (Jesus) for eternal life. He told Nicodemus that the way to enter the kingdom is through water (Jesus or living water) and Spirit (Holy Spirit).

Salvation is in drinking Jesus. Entering the kingdom requires birth by the living water and spirit. After we drink from Him the Holy Spirit descends upon us as He did Jesus at the river Jordan.

> *And Jesus when He was baptized went up straightway from the water: and lo, the heavens were opened unto him, and he saw the Spirit of God descending as a dove, and coming upon him.*
>
> MATTHEW 3:16

Jesus is offering living water to those who thirst for Him. He is not a philosophy, religion or formula. **The first time I tasted the living waters of Christ I was radically changed. I tried to survive on the waters of this world, and the more I drank the more I wanted. Wanting more of what did not satisfy in the first place consumed my life.** Finally, in my despair and emptiness, I cried out as a thirsty man would in the desert for water. Then and only then, I encountered the living water in the person of Jesus. One drink is all it took for me to know that He was the only one who could fill the desire of my soul.

One day I went for a walk in the desert. I wandered off the road fascinated by the beauty. Before long, I discovered I was lost. The thought of not having enough water made me thirsty. I tried to be calm, but my mind was relentless with images of thirst. Even though I had a canteen of water, it did not seem to satisfy my thirst. The more I drank, the thirstier I became. Finally, I recognized a landmark and found my way home. **However, the analogy of being lost in this life and drinking from the waters of this world without satisfaction is powerful indeed.**

Precious one, maybe you have not had this experience. Take the time to search your soul now for the truth. Have you tasted Jesus? Perhaps you are trying to fill your emptiness with more of the waters of this world. Do not let the devil lie to you any longer. **The waters of religion or secular knowledge will never satisfy your soul's yearning for the real thing.** In the name of Jesus, I implore you to cry out to Him now from the depths of your soul. Ask Him for a drink of His Water. He alone will satisfy you.

The process that Jesus describes below is the sequence we have been illustrating throughout our discussion.

Let the one who believes in me drink. As the scripture has said, Out of the believer's heart shall flow rivers of living water.

JOHN 7:38

The converted heart of man is a spring of refreshing revelation and resource for every human being. The more you consume, the larger the well becomes inside you, enabling others to drink. This is the design for real evangelism.

Jesus said to her, Go, call your husband, and come here.

The woman answered, I have no husband. Jesus said to her, you said well, I have no husband, for you have had five husbands; and he whom you now have is not your husband. This you have said truly.

The woman said to him, Sir, I perceive that you are a prophet.

Our fathers worshiped in this mountain, and you Jews say that in Jerusalem is the place where people ought to worship.

*Jesus said to her, Woman, **believe me**, the hour comes, when neither in this mountain, nor in Jerusalem, will you worship the Father.*

You worship that which you don't know. We worship that which we know; for salvation is from the Jews.

*But the hour comes, and **now is**, when the true worshippers will worship the Father in spirit and truth, for the Father seeks such to be his worshippers.*

God is spirit, and those who worship him must worship in spirit and truth.

The woman said to him, I know that Messiah comes, (he who is called Christ). When he has come, he will declare to us all things. Jesus said to her, I am he, the one who speaks to you.

JOHN 4:16–26

The woman wants what He is offering, so Jesus tests her. She passes the test and qualifies to taste the living water. The woman's honesty opens her heart to the Master.

She considered Jesus a prophet after He revealed her relationships with men. The interesting thing about prophecy is that it always works in harmony with worship. The subject of worship has been the topic of countless sermons. But it is important to note that it is not just singing. **My definition of worship is the outward expression of the inner knowledge or consciousness of Christ.**

Worship and the prophetic are heavenly tools that the Holy Ghost uses to install the wells of living water. Worship will break the rocks around stony hearts in order for surgery to occur. The heart transplant is necessary for the prophetic to operate in our lives. The heart of flesh, described in Ezekiel 11:19, will produce worship as living water to nourish, refresh and transform our lives.

Jesus did not condemn the woman, but instead prepared her for salvation because of her honesty. Therefore, Jesus decided to give her more water. Notice that living water gushed out in the form of revelation each time Jesus spoke. He said salvation is from the Jew. **He did not say** that it belonged only to them. Then He said the hour is **now** for the prophetic and worship to join with spirit and truth. God is spirit, and Jesus is truth. **Jesus is saying, in essence, that the worship the Father is looking for is those converted by living water. Their spirits and souls are one in Christ.** Do you see it? **Worship is a physical expression of the invisible conversion.**

Many churches today are preoccupied with the things in the future and miss the **now is** of the Spirit. This woman knew about the Messiah even though she was a heathen. As so many do, she had a preconceived idea of the way a Messiah should look and act. **We cannot afford to miss now, what we are looking for in the future.**

Jesus is saying, "if you have tasted my water you will begin to worship and the Father will visit you." Have you been visited by the Father? If not perhaps, you have not drunk from Jesus.

Then the woman put down her water-pot and went into the town, and said to the people,
Come and see a man who has been talking to me of everything I ever did! Is it possible that this is the Christ?
So they went out of the town and came to him.
While this was taking place, the disciples were saying to Jesus, Master, take some food.
But he said to them, I have food of which you have no knowledge.

> *So the disciples said one to another, Did anyone give
> him food?*
> *Jesus said, My food is to do the pleasure of him who sent
> me and to make his work complete.*
>
> JOHN 4:28–34

Look what happens when you taste Jesus. The woman leaves her natural resources in the form of her water pot and runs to tell her neighbors. Once she has the truth, she will tell others. If this has not happened in your life then chances are you have not drunk from Him.

Of course, the signs and wonders and the possibility that this could be the Messiah caused a great stir in the city. However, the woman was already manifesting the results of the living water in her life. She was worshiping God by talking about something that had touched her deeply. God is looking for those who worship Him in spirit and truth. **The level of our worship expresses our substance, reality and, ultimately, our belief**.

Meanwhile, Jesus turned His attention to His disciples to instruct them in the supernatural. **Remember, Jesus had asked for water initially and the disciples went to get food. However, Jesus never ate or drank during this encounter and the disciples were shocked**. Jesus was manifesting a kingdom principle: *blessed are those who hunger and thirst for righteousness, for they shall be completely satisfied.*

> *You would say, Four months from now is the time of
> the grain-cutting. Take a look, I say to you, at the fields;
> they are even now white for cutting.*
> *He who does the cutting now has his reward; he is get-
> ting together fruit for eternal life, so that he who did
> the planting and he who gets in the grain may have joy*

*together. In this the saying is a true one, One does the
planting, and another gets in the grain.*
**I sent you to get in grain, which you had no hand
in planting: other men did that work, and you
take the reward.**

JOHN 4:35–38

Jesus told His disciples the same thing He is saying today.
man's season and God's are different. Harvest is in the timing
of the Lord, not our calendars. The vision from heaven creates
both natural and spiritual supplies.

We have all heard messages about sowing and reaping.
This is a principle of the kingdom, without a doubt. But Jesus
is revealing a mystery to His disciples that we should understand as well.

**The love of the "Good Samaritan" (Luke 10:30–37) cap-
tured the Father's attention in such a way that He sent Jesus
to Samaria.** This act of compassion produced a harvest that
Jesus saw in the spirit realm, which is why He said *I sent you to
get in grain, which you had no hand in planting: other men did that
work, and you take the reward.* Chances are the Good Samaritan
was not even aware that his act of love was a prayer to the
Father to send forth laborers.

Jesus and His disciples were receiving the reward for this
man's love. Beloved, our seeds of love are eternal, and their
role in the destiny of our family and city can be dramatic. If we
will be obedient to the voice of the Holy Spirit and go when we
are sent, the fruit and rewards will be waiting.

*Then he said to them, "The harvest is indeed plentiful,
but the laborers are few. Pray therefore to the Lord of the
harvest, that he may send out laborers into his harvest.*

LUKE 10:2

The woman's testimony had created such hunger and thirst that revival broke out in this Samaritan city. Why? Because the woman had tasted the living water of Jesus, and **her worship was calling the Lord of the Harvest to send forth laborers**.

> *Many Samaritans in that city **believed** in Jesus because of the woman who said, He told me everything I've ever done.*
> *So when the Samaritans went to Jesus, they asked him to stay with them. He stayed in Samaria for two days. Many more Samaritans **believed** because of what Jesus said.*
> *And many more **believed**, because of His own word; And said to the woman, now we **believe**, not because of thy saying: for we have heard him ourselves, and know that this is indeed the Christ, the Savior of the world.*
>
> JOHN 4:39–44

The city was ripe for harvest because of the work of the Good Samaritan. In the story, the Samaritan man left the innkeeper two pennies to help with the expenses of the wounded man. The people of the city asked Jesus to stay two additional days to talk to them about the kingdom of God. The majesty of our Lord is beyond our traditional understanding. Jesus repaid the goodness of that Samaritan a thousand times more than his money.

BELIEVING IS A SIGN AND A WONDER

> *When he heard that Jesus had come from Judea to Galilee, he went and begged him to come down and heal his son, for he was at the point of death.*
> *Then Jesus said to him, "Unless you see signs and wonders you will not believe."*

The official said to him, "Sir, come down before my little boy dies."

*Jesus said to him, "Go; your son will live." The man **believed the word** that Jesus spoke to him and started on his way.*

As he was going down, his slaves met him and told him that his child was alive.

So he asked them the hour when he began to recover, and they said to him, "Yesterday at one in the afternoon the fever left him."

*The father **realized** that this was the hour when Jesus had said to him, "Your son will live." **So he himself believed**, along with his whole household.*

*Now this was the **second sign** that Jesus did after coming from Judea to Galilee.*

JOHN 4:49–54

John 4 demonstrates that **believing** is a **sign or miracle**. The only healing miracle described in the chapter concerns the son of the rich man in verse 50. Let us read together to understand the impact of this statement.

Jesus leaves the city and meets a nobleman whose son is at the point of death. He wants Jesus to come to his house and heal his son. Jesus then says, *"Unless you people see signs and wonders you will by no means believe."* Then He heals the son by His word and the nobleman **believed**. After he received confirmation of his son's recovery, the Bible says he **believed**. The Holy Ghost is revealing a powerful connection between faith and belief in the soul. The man had real faith, according to the scripture below.

Now faith is a well-grounded assurance of that for which we hope, and a conviction of the reality of things, which we do not see.

HEBREWS 11:1

115

When the father realized or became mentally conscious of his faith in Jesus his soul believed. Remember, we have demonstrated the difference between believing from a soul connected to our spirit and one who attempts to believe without that connection.

The last verse reveals the power of true believing. Read it. *(Now this was the second sign that Jesus did after coming from Judea to Galilee)*

The first recorded place that He stopped after leaving Judea was Samaria. There is no recorded healing or miracle in Samaria. The second miracle was the nobleman's son. This would indicate that the Samaritan woman's belief in Jesus was a miracle according to the scriptures.

In my judgment, true believing that transforms lives **is the believing** that the Holy Ghost is revealing through this verse. It is also the believing I have attempted to convey. The believing, which will transform your life and that of your nation, is from inside the mind of Christ. Unless the Holy Ghost converts our souls, we will not experience the wonders of the supernatural.

These powerful stories demonstrate the differences between salvation and entering the kingdom of God. Salvation is an ongoing process until our spirits and souls are one in the spirit and consciousness of Christ. The example that Jesus gave to Nicodemus is our model for being born into the kingdom, not reciting Romans 10:9-10.

Chapter Six

Divine Health

Now we have arrived at the place that will determine if this is just more information or the grace from heaven to set you free. Do you feel a fresh wind of the Spirit blowing through your consciousness? Do you hear that still, small voice encouraging you to believe in the supernatural? That voice will become louder and louder as your belief changes into faith.

The devil must know that you **know** Christ in a profoundly new way. The way to prove that is to stop responding to symptoms and suggestions from the devil.

The Lord will test us to see whom He can trust with the riches of His kingdom. Sickness and disease may be examples of such tests, in order to prove, whom we trust. The severity and duration of each test is dependant upon our level of trust. I am not implying God puts sickness or disease on persons. I am saying He will use the devil to test those who "**believe**" they are His children.

The miracle you have been asking God to perform in your life is within your reach. The reality of Christ in your life is changing what and how you believe. Beloved, your greatest victories have always been waiting on your decision to believe. Once you make **Christ a Reality** in your spirit, soul and body, nothing is impossible.

The following section will address two groups of people. The first group knows from a personal revelation, Christ as their Lord and desire to please Him above all else. The second group has not experienced a personal revelation of Jesus, even though they identify themselves Christians.

We trust physicians for our healing and health because of our conditioning. If our prayers do not "seem" to work, we run to the doctor. This behavior has negated our faith and grieved the Holy Spirit.

Those of us who love Jesus because we know Him must understand that He does not need doctors for our healing. We have all heard, from well-meaning men of God, that the Lord uses physicians to care for the sick. That statement applies to those who have not experienced Jesus as a reality in all of their being.

The Lord wants every human being to experience His love and majesty. Therefore, He will use anyone or anything to prolong a life, including physicians. Nevertheless, the ultimate goal of Christ is for each of us to depend on our Savior for everything, especially our health. If we depend on anyone else, Jesus is not our Lord.

The exchange of belief to faith is never more vivid than during an encounter with your physician. For example, you make an appointment with a doctor because of some illness. The appointment is your demonstration of hope or belief in the doctor's ability to relieve your pain. The physician asks some questions and measures your body temperature in order to make his diagnosis. Once the physician determines the cause for the illness, **your trust or belief is one with your faith.** Faith releases a temporary healing and crowns the doctors as the Lord of your body. If we go to a doctor to treat an ailment, regardless of the problem, we are telling Jesus that the cross is not enough.

One day, while reading the book of Daniel, the Lord spoke to me. He asked if I would be as bold as Shadrach would, Meshach and Abednego were in their belief. Therefore, I studied the third chapter, particularly their response to the king's threat of death if they did not bow to the golden idol.

> *Nebuchadnezzar said to them, "Is it true, O Shadrach, Meshach, and Abednego, that you do not serve my gods and you do not worship the golden statue that I have set up? Now if you are ready when you hear the sound of the horn, pipe, lyre, trigon, harp, drum, and entire musical ensemble to fall down and worship the statue that I have made, well and good. But if you do not worship, you shall immediately be thrown into a furnace of blazing fire, and **who is the god that will deliver you out of my hands?**" Shadrach, Meshach, and Abednego answered the king, "O Nebuchadnezzar, **we have no need to present a defense to you in this matter. If our God whom we serve is able to deliver us from the furnace of blazing fire and out of your hand, O king, let him deliver us. But if not, be it known to you, O king, that we will not serve your gods and we will not worship the golden statue that you have set up.**"*
>
> DANIEL 3:14–18

My immediate response was, "Of course, Jesus, I am ready to die for you." Then He asked, "Then why do you take medications and drugs?" I was shocked. It was something I had done all my life without even the slightest consideration that it was offending my Lord. The Holy Spirit said, "If you trust me to save your soul, am I not more than able to heal your body?"

I used those exact words when praying for the sick. However, it was not until the truth of that statement penetrated my spirit that I made the decision never to use prescription drugs or medications again.

The breakthrough that my wife experienced was truly a miracle. Like most people, she grew up believing that taking antibiotics and medications was not an offense to the Lord. One day, my example convicted her and she destroyed all of her medication as a statement of her faith. She had determined, as I had, that whether we lived or died we would not submit to using medications. Since that day, we have enjoyed the most marvelous supernatural health one can imagine. In fact, my wife's health has improved beyond her wildest expectations.

The truth is, there is not an antibiotic, chemotherapy or any other pill stronger than the wounds of our Savior. The power of His blood destroyed all disease, sickness or death. If you **know him,** you will know that. If you will say, "Jesus, your power is greater than any medicine because I know by experience you have delivered me and whether I live or die my life is yours." The faith in that statement will propel your miracle into manifestation. Why? Because the devil knows, he has lost his control of you through the fear of death.

Our breakthrough will never occur if we are not able to answer the way the Hebrews did in Daniel 3:17–18. Settle it now and forever. Regardless how the devil afflicts you, your knee will not bow nor your lips confess to any other God but Jesus.

If that is the foundation upon which your confidence and trust rests, the devil will flee. I did not say there would be no test or you would not go through the furnace of fire. You will. **However, on the other side of your victory, a new consciousness will materialize in you**. The knowledge that makes you the overcomer the devil fears will surface in you.

The instant you see your sickness or disease as an opportunity to advance in the kingdom of God, your deliverance

will begin. The power to believe in the supernatural will burst forth from your personal revelation of Christ. Your faith will withstand every assault the devil can mount, and more. You will begin to exercise your faith in the lives of those suffering round about you.

The truth is, the love of Christ will become your driving obsession to deliver the captives from death, hell and the grave. The more you love others by delivering them, the more command of the supernatural power you will possess.

I became convinced in every cell of my being that my Jesus was able to deliver me, **but even if He did not**, I was not going to bow to pharmakeia or any man made solution for my healing.

Pharmakeia *(far-mak-i´-ah)* is the Greek word that means medication ("pharmacy"), (by extension) magic (literally or figuratively), sorcery or witchcraft.

The root word is **pharmakeus** *(far-mak-yoos)*, from **pharmakon** (a drug, spell-giving potion); a druggist ("pharmacist") or poisoner, i.e. (by extension), a magician — sorcerer.

Pharmaceuticals work the same as traditional witchcraft. The drug provides relief from a symptom but corrupts the ability of the body's immune system to defend itself from the "spell-giving potion." The purpose of witchcraft is to replace the trust in God's divine plan of the cross with "man's system."

Today, physicians use a symbol of serpents on a pole constructed from the myth of the Greek god Asklepios. Satan is unable to create anything but confusion so he copies from the only one capable of creating, God. Moses obeyed God's instructions to reproduce a serpent on a pole to save the Israelites bitten by the serpents (Numbers 21:9).

The symbol that Moses was displaying illustrated the sin and death that Christ was to bear in order for all men to be set free from all sin, sickness and death. The emblem of medicine today empowers the curse Jesus bore, on all men who put their belief and trust in its authority.

I am not saying this to condemn those who are unable to fight because of the suffering and pain in your bodies. You must begin at the level of your faith. Study the scriptures; see how ordinary men became extraordinary through dying to this world's beliefs and **believing** Jesus.

Israel lived 450 years free of disease through the covenant of divine healing established in Exodus 15:26.

> *And he said, If with all your heart you will give attention to the voice of the Lord your God, and do what is right in his eyes, giving ear to his orders and keeping his laws, I will not put on you any of the diseases which I put on the Egyptians: for I am the Lord your life-giver.*

No other culture in the world possessed the healing power of Israel. There is no record of this power in Egypt, India or China. The Hebrews alone received this privilege from Abraham onward until Asa, the king who broke the covenant by trusting in physicians.

> *In the thirty-ninth year of his reign, Asa got a foot disease that became progressively worse. Instead of asking the Lord for help, he went to doctors.*
>
> 2 CHRONICLES 16:12

You may be in a battle for your very life right now and have heard physicians tell you unless you take this drug or that; you are not going to live. I will simply tell you what Jesus said, and is saying: *All Things Are Possible to Him Who Believes.*

The word "**believes**" is very significant. It means continually, on going. You must win the battle each day over your mind and emotions. **The reason that the devil brings you**

symptoms is so you will believe the lie and lose the battle.
Symptoms are an illusion. The way that a magician uses illu-
sions to make you believe a trick is the same method the devil
uses. We must have the mind of Christ in order not to fall for
the deceptions of the enemy.

The devil, on occasions, creates symptoms for me in order
to measure my response. The louder I laugh, the more humili-
ated he becomes. You must know something about your enemy.
He is full of pride and does not like to be embarrassed in front
of his demons. Settle it forever. If you belong to Jesus completely **He** will take care of you. If there are areas in your life,
such as unforgiveness or other sin that requires your repentance, then ask forgiveness now.

Jesus has given us all the power necessary to overcome
everything in this world. This statement must be more than
words if you are to win the battle each day for your health.

Whichever part of our being we trust to man makes us
vulnerable in that area. The commitment of our whole body to
the will of God is the mind of Christ. Healing in any depart-
ment of our nature is but a means to an end. The purpose
for healing is health, abiding health for our bodies, souls and
spirits.

In my opinion, the greatest battle ahead for the Church
will be in health and healing. Praise the Lord for the men and
women of God who are delivering countless thousands around
the world from the miseries of affliction. **I am forever grate-**
ful to the Lord for the privilege to pray for the sick and then
witness miracles and healings. I believe it is our heritage
as believers and the more conscious of Christ we become
greater miracles will be the result.

God created the body of man to house the Holy Ghost.
The soul and body are the weakest points of man. The devil is
aware of that and as a result, it is the place of our greatest trials
and tribulations.

One of the goals of this book is to train true believers in spirit, soul and body. **My prayer is for this clarion call to provoke a holy anger in my fellow servants to resist the devil in sickness the same way we resist him in sin.**

Healing is in degrees, based on two conditions. The first is the amount of healing virtue released. The definition of virtue is spiritual energy. In the account of the woman with the issue of blood, Jesus was aware when virtue left His body.

> *Immediately aware that power had gone forth from him, Jesus turned about in the crowd and said, "Who touched my clothes?"*
>
> MARK 5:30

The second condition is the amount of faith mixed with the virtue. These two invisible forces create tangible results.

The author of Hebrews affirms this thought:

> *...but the word of the report did not profit them, not being mixed with faith in those who heard.*
>
> HEBREWS 4:2

Healing is in three planes: spirit healing, soul healing and body healing. The person sick in his body is sick in his spirit first. Sickness then travels through the soul and finally manifests in the body.

My greatest successes in healings occurred when I finally understood how my body responds to my spirit. The reality of that statement became truth for me a few years ago when I was ill. A man of God came to visit me. This man had a victorious spirit that was contagious. He began to talk about the Lord in a way that I could tangibly feel like a cold drink of water. My spirit was dry and thirsty and began to respond to the living water coming from this man. The way that the woman at the well drank from Jesus is the same way I drank. I received my healing before he left.

This man carried a consciousness of divine health, and my spirit drank the substance or virtue. That virtue mixed with my faith even as anemic as it was, and healing was the result. It was as if my spirit was malnourished and this man had intravenously fed me a steak. **In essence, his spirit's connection to the Holy Spirit fed my spirit, which in turn released virtue throughout my body.**

The healing of our spirit merges the spirit of man to God eternally. The healing of the soul mends mental disorders and carries harmony and peace by the mind of Christ. Finally, physical healing completes the union of man with God through the Holy Spirit.

My wife has written a book called *Iniquity,* which will help you to discover areas in your spirit and soul that have hindered your healing.

HOW TO STOP TAKING YOUR MEDICINE

MIRACLES AND DIVINE HEALTH

Divine healing is the removal of the disease in the body by the power of God. It is the life of God transmitted into our beings either from heaven or through another man of faith. Divine health is to live day-by-day and hour-by-hour in touch with God, so that the life of God flows into the body just as the life of God flows into the mind or spirit.

A miracle is the creative action by the Spirit of God. The salvation of souls is a divine miracle of God. God created all the organs of man from a spiritual design. For example, the physical heart is different from the spiritual but both are important for life. God made man from His image and used the material of the earth to hold His glory. Adam became a living being after God breathed His Spirit into him.

Sin corrupts man beginning with his spirit and passing through the soul into the bodily organs. **In order to release healing and miracles into these clay vessels, the Holy Ghost breathes life into the lifeless areas. The more we believe the invisible, the greater the result.**

> *Or do you not know that your body is a temple of the Holy Spirit within you, which you have from God, and that you are not your own?*
> *For you were bought with a price; therefore glorify God in your body.*
>
> 1 CORINTHIANS 6:19–20

People are sick for the same reason that they sin. They surrender to the suggestion of the thing that is evil, and it takes possession of the heart. So, when the suggestion of sickness approaches in any form, cast it away as evil.

For example, how would you feel if when you arrived at your new home, which cost thousands of dollars, you were greeted with the horrible smell of rotting dead animals?

This is an analogy of our bodies if we allow unclean thoughts, to not only inhabit but also to die and decay. Cancer, heart, liver, blood disease and death are all results of unclean thoughts. This is a product of our mental and spiritual condition built through fear, mental structures, guilt, iniquity, curses and **unbelief.**

We have already said that the real healing in our life begins in our spirits.

> *Wherefore also he is able to save to the uttermost them that draw near unto God through him, seeing he ever lives to make intercession for them.*
>
> HEBREWS 7:25

Two words stand out in this scripture for us to understand. The word **save** can be translated **heal** and the word **uttermost** means that nothing can prevent the grace of God from reaching it. That should settle it in our souls forever. **Our action towards God determines our healing. Once the salvation begins in our spirits nothing, and I mean nothing, has the power to stop His virtue except our refusal to believe.**

It does not matter how beautiful our lamps are if they do not produce light. If the fuse is blown, and there is no electricity passing through the wires, the result will be no light. Our spirits work the same way as fuses. The Holy Ghost is the power from heaven enabling us with virtue and faith. Unbelief is the result of "blown fuses."

The essence of the Christ consciousness is in the joining of believing with faith. The centers of our heart, soul and mind connected with our spirits enjoined by the Holy Ghost create an explosion throughout our beings. The Holy Ghost connected to our spirits is equal to converting our electricity from 110 volts to 220. The power does not just double but exponentially increases in speed, frequency and amount.

The faith that permeates your whole being feels like lightning inside your body. I have experienced this sensation on several occasions, and each time my faith has no limits. I feel as though I could believe for anything and it would happen. This is the connection of the Spirit of God with our whole being. Jesus maintained this power because of His oneness with His Father and the Holy Ghost.

One of the most powerful realizations we must have in Christ is once we are free from iniquity and sin; our bodies are free from sickness. Sin is defined as actions and thoughts not birthed by faith. (*Whatever is not of faith is sin;* Romans 14:23)

The proof is in the scripture below.

*And Jesus **seeing their faith** said to the paralytic, my son, your sins are forgiven.*

127

But there were some of the scribes sitting there and reasoning in their hearts,

Why does this man speak that way? He is blaspheming; who can forgive sins but God alone?

And immediately Jesus, aware in His spirit that they were reasoning that way within themselves, said to them, why are you reasoning about these things in your hearts?

Which is easier, to say to the paralytic, Your sins are forgiven; or to say, Arise, and take up your pallet and walk?

But in order that you may know that the Son of Man has authority on earth to forgive sins — He said to the paralytic —

I say to you, rise, take up your pallet and go home.

And he rose and immediately took up the pallet and went out in the sight of all; so that they were all amazed and were glorifying God, saying, We have never seen anything like this.

MARK 2:5–12

The same faith that saved this man healed his body. The Church today, for the most part, understands the authority God has over sin for salvation. However, are very doubtful and inexperienced in the power of God.

One thing that has discredited the healing ministries is the numbers of people who do not receive their miracles after prayer. Generally, if they pray for ten people maybe only one or two receive their healing. The rest will receive perhaps a portion of the power of God necessary for recovery.

This did not occur with Jesus, of course, Jesus contained the Holy Spirit without measure. Nevertheless, if these same ministries would remain and not stop praying, I believe the miracles would dramatically increase. Unfortunately, men instead of God schedule healing campaigns.

However, the same is true in salvation. Perhaps two out of ten persons may have a revelation of Christ in their souls. That revelation can open heaven temporarily for him to experience God as his Father. The only hindrance is unbelief and sin blocking man's consciousness.

Real healing has a progressive path. Once the spirit of man is touched with the virtue of God, our responsibility begins in earnest. At that point, our spirits must not rest until the Holy Ghost consumes our every thought. We have said it so many times throughout this book, but it is worth repeating: We must be just like Jesus in spirit, soul and body. In other words, we must possess His consciousness — all of it.

The answers to these questions will expose your level of His consciousness. Do you take medication? Are you fearful? Are you pursuing money? Are you offended easily? Do you trust anyone or anything more than the word of God?

If your answer is yes to any of these questions, your spirit will have little if any authority over illness. I have good news, though. You do not have to remain powerless over sin, sickness and disease. The minute you begin to order your priorities to consume His word, the sooner your spirit will begin to empower you.

My life changed dramatically when I realized my soul and body were spiritually anemic. I began to fast from solid food and feed on spiritual food all day and sometimes into the early morning hours. The first thing I did was reread the Bible from Genesis to Revelation. My encounters with the Holy Spirit went from occasional to constant. His voice became louder and louder until the voices of doubt and unbelief in my soul were hardly noticeable. Within weeks, the parables of the Bible were being lived in my consciousness. I saw myself walking down the path with Jesus when He cursed the fig tree. I could see Lazarus wrapped in grave clothes hopping out of the cave and so on.

My spirit was regaining the authority over my mind and body. I replaced images I once had of fear and skepticism with knowledge not describable by words. The invisible became visible as I spoke.

For example, my son was suffering with an ear infection and high temperature. I saw myself standing in his room but I looked much larger than my natural appearance. As I walked into the room, the spirit hovering over my son began to shake as if terrified. I said, "you filthy devil leave his body at once." Before I finished that statement the spirit left, and my son's temperature became normal immediately.

From that day until now, I have been diligent in practicing several things. First, each day I spend time in the word of God. Spiritual food is vital for stamina and revelation. **Revelation is the greatest proof that you are in contact with the Holy Ghost.**

Second, it is important to have communion in the form of prayer, the Lord's Supper and quiet meditation. Becoming one with Him is done in the secret place where there is no distraction. The secret place is secret because it must be discovered each time you enter.

Third, it is imperative to talk to real believers and share the goodness of the Lord in your life. The Spirit needs a human voice to tell others of His nature and character. Therefore, if you make yourself a living, speaking testimony of His wonders, faith will grow in your life and inspire others.

The point I am making is that our healing is as certain as our salvation. However, we will not receive what Jesus purchased for us if our belief systems have become unbelief and doubt. It would be like someone having one billion dollars in a bank but unable to withdraw it because of unbelief.

The same unbelief is hindering us from withdrawing all that Jesus deposited to us who **believe.** Information is necessary in the beginning to point someone to the cross. However, after that, **Believing is the tool of the Holy Ghost to keep us connected to Him.**

If your spirit is at the place where it has no appetite for spiritual things, you are an easy target for the devil. You will never get your physical healing until you receive a spiritual one. That is why so many Christians go to doctors. They would rather put their faith and trust in a physician instead of Jesus. Nevertheless, if you get your healing by the Spirit and keep your connection fresh and vibrant through the steps we spoke about, you will live in divine health and never need doctors again.

Once you have become truly one with Christ, in spirit, soul and body disease will fall off your body like the scales did from Paul's eyes. The consciousness of Christ will not allow anything unholy to prosper in our life.

In fact, nothing from that realm will come within miles of you. How close do you think evil could get to Jesus? Nothing will approach you unless your spirit becomes weak. Keep your spirit strong, and your soul and body will live in divine health.

The proof that your spirit and soul are in Christ is divine health. The final step is ours. Jesus has done everything necessary to provide it. Will you be like the father of the epileptic who cried, "I believe but help my unbelief?" Believing Jesus will change the reality you are now living.

Let me pray for you.

Jesus, it is my heart's desire that you touch each person who reads this book with a visible miracle manifestation. If they are sick, heal them. If they are depressed, deliver them. If they are broke, send finances. Whatever their need, I am asking you by your mercy and grace to honor my request with a miracle in their lives. Not to glorify me, God forbid, but to honor your word that you have given me to deliver. Jesus, I give you the glory and honor for everything you have done and will do through these revelations.

Figure 1

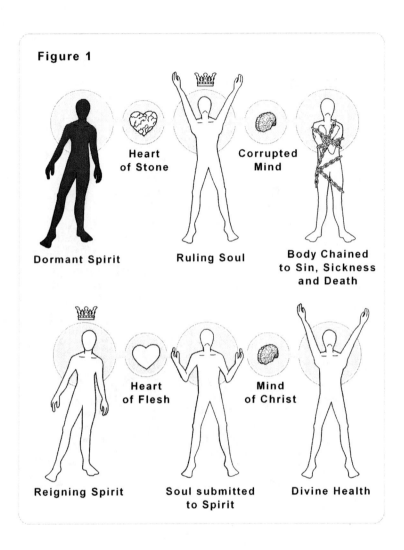

Figure 2

Descriptions of Man's Centers
Each center is created spiritually except the body

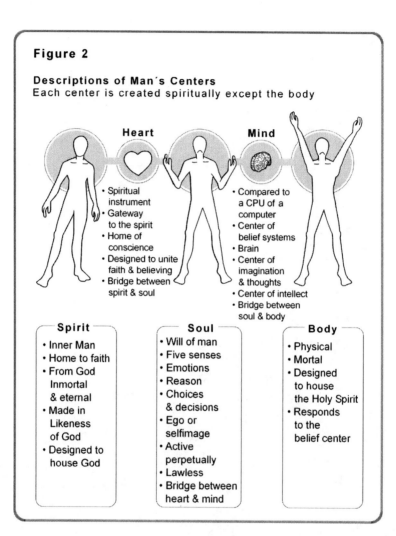

Heart
- Spiritual instrument
- Gateway to the spirit
- Home of conscience
- Designed to unite faith & believing
- Bridge between spirit & soul

Mind
- Compared to a CPU of a computer
- Center of belief systems
- Brain
- Center of imagination & thoughts
- Center of intellect
- Bridge between soul & body

Spirit
- Inner Man
- Home to faith
- From God Inmortal & eternal
- Made in Likeness of God
- Designed to house God

Soul
- Will of man
- Five senses
- Emotions
- Reason
- Choices & decisions
- Ego or selfimage
- Active perpetually
- Lawless
- Bridge between heart & mind

Body
- Physical
- Mortal
- Designed to house the Holy Spirit
- Responds to the belief center

Conclusion

The substances of all things are in and of Christ. Those who live outside this knowledge will continually be at the mercy of the devil. Christ is the kingdom of God, and those who enter His kingdom must be immersed in His Spirit and consciousness.

The reality we are living is the result of the kingdom in which we believe. We may say one thing with our mouths, but live our lives completely different. This is the result of the substance inside our souls.

The Holy Spirit designed this book to open the eyes of those who are tired of saying one thing and experiencing something else. Our belief system will change when the Spirit consumes the substance inside us. This is not a cliché, but a reality.

There are no shortcuts to living in the Spirit. If we truly want power in our life over every devil and disease, we must have the mind of the one who overcame everything.

*I have said all these things to you so that in me you
may have peace. In the world you have trouble: but take
heart! I have overcome the world.*

JOHN 16:33

The consciousness of Christ is not a fancy phrase meant to
sound ethereal. It is the reality of becoming one with God. The
method is the same for me as it was for Jesus: death to this life,
which is the definition of a disciple, then baptism in order to be
raised in the image of Christ.

**One of the greatest lessons I learned was changing my
trials into training. The day I learned that God was using
the devil as His personal whipping boy to train those He
loves, my consciousness began to change. I purposed to use
the power of love to bring my soul and mind under submission. I no longer fought to preserve my reality but submitted
to learn His. His substance began to grow in me and allowed
me to supernaturally believe for all things.**

Today, the consciousness of Christ is growing in me proportionate to my submission to the sanctification of the Holy
Ghost. I am able to connect my spirit with my soul to believe
and witness amazing breakthroughs.

If you are not experiencing the righteousness, joy and
peace of Christ in your spirit, soul and body, you have not
entered the invisible and powerful kingdom of God. The way
to enter is to drink the living water Jesus is offering right now.
Allow that water to transform you, beginning with your spirit
and working through your soul.

"You must be born of water and Spirit," Jesus told Nicodemus.
Baptism by the Spirit occurs only when washed in the water of
the word. *"Now ye are clean through the word, which I have spoken
unto you."*

When this occurs, believing is one with our spirit and
joined to the Holy Ghost. **The Christ consciousness replaces**

the sin consciousness along with any doubt and unbelief. Heavenly experiences alter our present reality. Heaven contains no sickness, disease, death or devil.

The life you are living today does not have to be the life you live tomorrow. Make a decision to change your belief systems. Ask the Holy Spirit what you should do, and be prepared to follow Him to the wilderness to change. If you will make that decision, your life will change.

There is no conclusion to believing in the manner of Jesus. My greatest prayer is to witness a generation whose experience of the supernatural converts manifestations of signs and wonders into permanent habitations. This restoration of the kingdom will usher in King Jesus. Miracles, signs and wonders have never changed a nation but believing supernaturally will. If the supernatural life is the source by which the believer conducts his or her life, heaven will have taken up residence on planet earth. Then the prayer that Jesus taught His disciples to pray will have manifested. *"Thy reign come: Thy will come to pass, as in heaven also on the earth"* (Matthew 6:10.)

Heaven has been waiting on us to exercise our dominion and authority with the knowledge of Christ. We have nothing to lose and everything to gain.

Amen

Appendix

Health tips that have worked in my life

Today, most people are addicted to a diet that is responsible for most of the health problems in the world. Regardless of one's socioeconomic background, the habitual eating of wrong foods is the result of wrong beliefs.

Most people would rather believe advertisements about foods that promise good taste than listen to the Spirit on the proper foods to eat. Consuming processed foods and sugars contaminates our sense of taste from childhood. Therefore, the foods, which are least appealing, are generally the ones required for proper health.

The Lord is concerned about our bodies because they are the temporal home from which He conducts kingdom business. Therefore, He knows what fuel each of us should consume to operate at maximum efficiency. The analogy of putting kerosene in your automobile instead of gasoline is an appropriate one.

Many Christians and non-Christians have written books describing the benefits of eating properly. It is not my intention to write a health book. My purpose is to give those who are suffering in their bodies some simple natural remedies. These cures have aided our family in removing the symptoms created by wrong food choices.

As we discovered in this book, all sickness and disease originate in our spirits and are the result of sin. Until the Holy Spirit sanctifies our spirit, soul and body we will all encounter symptoms of diseases in our bodies. Therefore, in order to allow the Holy Spirit to complete His work, I have discovered some simple things to reduce ailments and infirmities resulting from our bodies' imbalance.

For example if I experience symptoms resembling influenza such as a runny nose, fevers or body aches, I immediately consume vitamin C. The amount I consume is five to six grams of pure ascorbic acid every four hours until the symptoms leave. Too much Vitamin C can produce a side effect of temporary diarrhea.

Through fasting, I discovered many secrets for healing and the path to divine health. For instance, the Lord said, "many illnesses are the result of dehydration, lack of fresh air and sunlight." Therefore, I attempt to consume a gallon of fresh water a day along with walking outside in the sun. The truth is, the human body will heal itself through proper nutrition and physical exercise.

Fasting is a great tool for detoxification and spiritual cleansing. In addition, fasting allows the Holy Spirit to instruct us in temple maintenance after the fast. We learned to take papaya for any nausea and green tea instead of coffee. We avoid eating white sugar and foods that produce yeast. We also eliminated pork and seafood that does not have scales and gills. Those simple steps have helped us to maintain a healthy body while the Holy Spirit sanctifies our complete being.

The most important thing I learned from fasting was that the less food I consumed in the natural state, the more

**food I received in my spirit; the net effect was divine health
in my spirit, soul and body.**

Do not be condemned by the devil for using the hospital or physicians in emergencies. For instance, if someone is involved in a car accident, trust the Lord to provide a doctor to handle your immediate needs. I do not recommend surgery but each person must trust Jesus at the level you have obtained. Remember the story in Daniel concerning Shadrach, Meshach and Abednego.

Finally, trust the Holy Spirit for all your needs, especially your health, and you will be free from accidents. Paul was beaten, stoned and sent a thorn in the flesh (2 Corinthians 12:6–12). The Lord told Paul that His "Grace" was sufficient for Paul.

In order for us to overcome, we must know the meaning of grace beyond the "unmerited favor" definition. Grace is the supernatural power released through the resurrection of Christ to **know the truth**.

> *For the law was given by Moses, but grace and truth
> came by Jesus Christ.*
>
> JOHN 1:17

The truth is a person, Christ. The truth is flesh when we live inside of Jesus. This is possible because of the grace that He provided for us. Christ never lived in fear of accidents, sickness, disease, or death. Jesus is waiting to open the door to the supernatural. **If you believe it, you will live it.**

International

A book that will take you to
experience the depths within the
invisible kingdom of God.

Discover what is the major hindrance,
that is stopping you from entering the
glorious manifestations of God.

The answers to many of the difficult
questions concerning spiritual warfare.
A book of wisdom and experience
from a General in war.

Discover the strategies to defeat
your finances greater thief,
the spirit of Mammon.